UPRISING

UPRISING
AN ANCIENT PROPHET'S SACRED WORDS FOR MODERN ACTIVISTS

BY STEPHEN FEITH

EQUIP PRESS

To Quinn, Elijah, & Oliver,
always stay humble and kind.

You each personify the best of what I could ever offer the world, and yet you all can offer the world so much more than I ever will. My prayer for you three is to, like Jesus, grow "in wisdom and in stature and in favor with God and all the people" (Luke 2:52).

CONTENTS

UPRISING

In 1979, an airplane carrying 257 people from more than half a dozen different countries left Auckland, New Zealand, for a sightseeing trip to Antarctica. These day trips were both relatively new to the public and very expensive. This was long before people could easily access live satellite images of the southern pole in high-resolution photos and videos from a device that fits in their pocket.

It was the first time Captain Jim Collins and his copilot, Greg Cassin, made this flight; however, both were sufficiently experienced and qualified. Tragically, neither knew that there was a two-degree error in the flight plan they were given the morning of the trip. Those incorrect coordinates placed them 28 miles to the east of where Collins and Cassin thought they would be—unknowingly heading directly toward a 12,000-foot volcano.

The pilots descended the plane to an altitude of 2,000 feet to give passengers a better view of the landscape. Clouds in the sky blended in with the snow on the ground so that neither pilot could tell the difference between the two. Not long after that, the plane crashed into the side of Mount Erebus. Everyone on board was killed instantly.

Seconds before Flight 901 made its fateful impact

nearly 50 years ago, the plane's ground proximity warning system began sounding alarms. The instructions were clear: "Whoop, whoop. Pull up!" But by then, it was too late for anyone to do anything. Had the warnings occurred sooner, Collins and Cassin would have certainly been able to save the lives of everyone on their aircraft.

It is one of the deadliest aircraft accidents in history—caused by a seemingly insignificant error. Since then, pilots have been taught the 1 in 60 rule. The rule states that for every degree a plane veers off its course, it misses its intended target by one mile for every 60 miles it flies. The point is that a small margin of error becomes a major, potentially dangerous issue the longer it goes unaddressed.

For example, a plane a couple of degrees off its path would miss the airport in Milwaukee only by a mile if it were flying from Madison, Wisconsin. However, a plane traveling from Las Vegas to Madison would miss all of Dane County at just two degrees off route.

Once off course, the fix isn't to adjust by one or two degrees. Since a mistake has already been made, the correction will need to be three, four, or more degrees depending on how long and far off the target it has been. If the pilots found out halfway through the flight that they were four degrees off since takeoff from Las Vegas, they would need to course correct by eight degrees given the amount of time left on the flight to Madison.

"WHOOP, WHOOP! PULL UP!"

Now, most of you aren't interested in air navigation or reading about math, so let's move on. I begin with this tragic story because it highlights what can happen to all of us in any aspect of our lives, including spiritually. Even when we start off the right way with our faith, staying on track is just as, if not more, critical. Whether we're aware of it or not, drifting is going to happen. The results can be spiritually fatal.

And in our society, followers of Jesus are off course.

Many of us live in a culture that has championed the ambiguity of truth. It has been stated often that there are no absolute truths—which is, paradoxically, an absolute truth. When I was studying *Jude* years before 2020, I couldn't imagine the chaos and confusion that would ensue with masks, vaccines, shut-downs, elections, and more amongst believers.

We should have recognized the truth better than most. After all, Jesus claimed he was and is "the truth" (John 14:6). But we didn't. We got off the path at some point and chased after something else instead of Jesus. Atlanta-area pastor, Andy Stanley, seems to agree. He writes, "The political, social, economic, and health crises of 2020 didn't cause us to misprioritize our values. These events simply exposed what's been true for a long time."[1]

Whatever we collectively valued and pursued, it wasn't *the Truth*.

When we get off our path, we have several choices. We can make a change now. This is most preferred. We can procrastinate until we have to make a big turn later. Worst of all, we can continue to drift until there's a fatal blow we don't see coming. This makes Jude's message as urgent as it is important today as we seek to get back on track. He's sounding the alarm: "Whoop, whoop! Pull up!"

This book isn't a plea to go back to a time before post-modern philosophy but an urge to transcend the rote debates taking place everywhere, from nationally televised presidential debates to private conversations around dining room tables over the holidays. In thoroughly studying *Jude*, we will find significantly impactful ways to move onward meaningfully.

UPRISING

For the typical reader of the Bible, *Jude* might be, as one theologian titled an article he wrote, "The Most Neglected Book in the New Testament."[2] *Jude* is the second-to-last work in our New Testament. It is one of the shortest "books" in both Testaments but doesn't get read often, if ever, by many despite that.

This likely has to do with the frequent references to mostly unfamiliar parts of the Old Testament and Hebrew folklore throughout this brief text. It made sense to mention those stories thousands of years ago because Jude's original audience would have been Jewish Christians. They understood, with little to no explanation, those references and their implications.

For many of us today, though, we need help finding trustworthy background information for *1 Enoch* and the allusions to the *Testament of Moses*. As such, many readers skim over *Jude* with intentions and plan to figure out its meanings later.

We're just some of those who have had a difficult time understanding *Jude*. While accepted by his peers and early churches, his letter was eventually contested by some influential theologians. Those who objected to including Jude in the New Testament were still determining if it even met the criteria for being included because of his use of those confusing pseudepigraphal texts!

BAD NEWS

There may be another, yet less apparent, reason that those of us who have read *Jude* haven't studied it beyond a reading: Jude directly confronts problems in the community of believers. He warns of eternal separation from God if changes aren't made.

Both *sin* and *hell* are topics that most of us living in the 21st century would prefer never to talk about. We'd rather listen to something "positive and encouraging" on the local Christian radio station. (Granted, some would prefer to *always* talk about sin and hell, but that doesn't describe Jude, who admits he does so *reluctantly*.)

We need to be confronted with the truth regarding the lies deeply woven into our society's fabric. There's more going on than memes being shared and misin-formation going viral daily. These snippets don't just affect the way we think. They affect the behaviors of people and groups of people.

Consider the actions that some thousands of people took on January 6, 2021, because of their firmly held beliefs that the 2020 presidential election was inter-fered with. Despite many investigations showing no evidence of widespread voter fraud, people got on buses to travel to Washington D.C. to protest and declare, "Stop the Steal," and overturn the election results.

Disturbingly, some in those crowds were seen carrying the hangman's knot while others held the Christian cross. Both were used to cause death at one point, but today, one symbolizes love and the other hate. That's why I bring this event up now.

With a large number involved and only unproven claims and conspiracy theories to go off, people on both sides of the conflict had their lives taken from them at our nation's capital that day. Countless others working at the capitol building that day have been dealing with post-traumatic stress disorder since then, with at least four dying by suicide.

When deception goes unchallenged, death follows. Author Leonard Sweet writes about the connections between evil, the devil, and lies: "Evil and devil are basi-cally the same word... that literally means one who spreads false reports, one who slanders and defames and casts aspersions, one who lies, and thus divides people from one another. The devil is the slanderer and the divider, the libeler and the liar."**3**

Jesus called this very thing out while on earth with his disciples 2,000 years ago. John 10:10 plainly states the critical differences between Jesus' purpose and the devil's: "The thief's purpose is to steal and kill and destroy. My purpose is to give them a rich and satisfying life." This is a strong filter for us when we're unsure whether something is from God. It's also convicting. Do we cling to the cross or wave the knot?

GOOD NEWS

Now, you can put down this book and never pick it up again, declaring its content to be "fake news." (That's *not* the good news.) Doing so will only delay what really needs to happen in our lives. We need hard conversations about the issues we're facing before those issues will get better. Moving believers from spiritual spectators to faithful activists is what Jude dared to write about.

He is writing to fellow believers, people not all that different from you and me. (*This* is the good news.) Starting with this: Jude offers readers several reasons for substantial hope.

First, Jude assures readers of our salvation and God's love for us. God's love and redemption are readily available to us no matter where we come from, what we've done, or who we are. This is the truth of our identities and our faith and is our baseline for reality in a world that doesn't always know how to discern what's true and what's not.

Then, while Jude warns about the attitudes and behaviors of those who do harm, we can extract the foundations and applications of truth. We must activate these disciplines in our lives to ensure that our faith flourishes no matter what.

Finally, Jude concludes by proclaiming we will have an eternity together with our loving God if we persevere. He assures victory for those who remain faithful. Having confirmed who we are and warned whom to look out for, Jude points out that we're not merely to settle with getting by. The Christian life is supposed to be a real, eternal, and better life than we've ever dreamed of.

That's the impact of truth in our lives.

Throughout this book, I'll share several stories that occurred over a few *long* years in my own life. I made a lot of mistakes and experienced heartbreak that could have been avoided if I had studied *Jude* sooner. It was a critical time in my life, and Jude's teachings could've made a real difference in my life had I put them into practice sooner.

JESUS' LITTLE BROTHER, JUDE

Before we go any further, let's become acquainted with the author of this biblical text. We can learn a lot about people by how they introduce themselves.

Many spend meticulous time on their Twitter bios to make them stand out from other profiles so that they might attract more followers. I spent some time trying to develop an attractive biography to establish my credibility in writing such a book as this!

However, Jude simply describes himself as a "slave of Jesus Christ" and "brother of James" before transitioning to the reason he's writing (**Jude 1**). In doing so, he expresses humility while establishing his authority to write. By being the brother of James, believed to be the key leader of the church in Jerusalem, this Jude is not just a slave to, but also the brother of, Jesus. This is supported by what we read in Mark when those trying to discredit Jesus mention his siblings by name:

> "He's [Jesus] just a carpenter—Mary's boy. We've known him since he was a kid. We know his brothers, James, Justus, Jude, Simon, and his sisters. Who does he think he is?"

> **Mark 6:3 (MSG)**

Funny enough, the first time we read about Jude in the biblical texts, people are saying Jesus can't be who he claims to be because of who they know his brother, Jude, to be. But now, Jesus' brother finds himself on the frontlines of his Lord's mission.

THE EPISTLE OF JUDE

As we set off on this journey, we must keep in mind and be aware that most of the people who initially received this letter could not read it. The content was sent in written form but would have been read out loud when it arrived. Therefore, the recipients would have heard the message from someone reading it aloud instead of reading it themselves.

In this sense, it was originally received similarly to how we hear a message or sermon at a church gathering on a Sunday. It's meant to invoke emotion as Jude presents his arguments. I suggest you read Jude's words, at least in part, the way his original hearers would've for maximum impact.

As we go forward, I pray for you what Jude prayed for you: "May God give you more and more mercy, peace, and love" (**Jude 1**). As we walk with Jesus into whatever is next for each of us, may we go in mercy, peace, and love.

THE LETTER
OF JUDE

This letter is from Jude, a slave of
Jesus Christ and a brother of James.

I am writing to all who have been called
by God the Father, who loves you and
keeps you safe in the care of Jesus Christ.

May God give you more and
more mercy, peace, and love.

Dear friends, I had been eagerly planning
to write to you about the salvation we
all share. But now I find that I must
write about something else, urging
you to defend the faith that God has
entrusted once for all time to his holy
people. I say this because some ungodly
people have wormed their way into your
churches, saying that God's marvelous
grace allows us to live immoral lives.
The condemnation of such people was
recorded long ago, for they have denied
our only Master and Lord, Jesus Christ.

So I want to remind you, though you
already know these things, that Jesus first

rescued the nation of Israel from Egypt, but later he destroyed those who did not remain faithful. And I remind you of the angels who did not stay within the limits of authority God gave them but left the place where they belonged. God has kept them securely chained in prisons of darkness, waiting for the great day of judgment. And don't forget Sodom and Gomorrah and their neighboring towns, which were filled with immorality and every kind of sexual perversion. Those cities were destroyed by fire and serve as a warning of the eternal fire of God's judgment.

In the same way, these people—who claim authority from their dreams—live immoral lives, defy authority, and scoff at supernatural beings. But even Michael, one of the mightiest of the angels, did not dare accuse the devil of blasphemy, but simply said, "The Lord rebuke you!" (This took place when Michael was arguing with the devil about Moses' body.) But these people scoff at things they do not understand. Like unthinking animals, they do whatever their instincts tell them, and so they bring about their own destruction. What sorrow awaits them! For they follow in the footsteps of Cain, who killed his brother. Like Balaam, they deceive people for money. And like Korah, they perish in their rebellion.

When these people eat with you in your fellowship meals commemorating the Lord's love, they are like dangerous reefs that can shipwreck you. They are like shameless shepherds who care only for themselves. They are like clouds blowing over the land without giving any rain. They are like trees in autumn that are doubly dead, for they bear no fruit and have been pulled up by the roots. They are like wild waves of the sea, churning up the foam of their shameful deeds. They are like wandering stars, doomed forever to blackest darkness.

Enoch, who lived in the seventh generation after Adam, prophesied about these people. He said, "Listen! The Lord is coming with countless thousands of his holy ones to execute judgment on the people of the world. He will convict every person of all the ungodly things they have done and for all the insults that ungodly sinners have spoken against him."

These people are grumblers and complainers, living only to satisfy their desires. They brag loudly about themselves, and they flatter others to get what they want.

But you, my dear friends, must remember what the apostles of our Lord Jesus Christ predicted. They told you that in the last

times there would be scoffers whose
purpose in life is to satisfy their ungodly
desires. These people are the ones who
are creating divisions among you. They
follow their natural instincts because
they do not have God's Spirit in them.

But you, dear friends, must build each
other up in your most holy faith, pray in
the power of the Holy Spirit, and await
the mercy of our Lord Jesus Christ, who
will bring you eternal life. In this way, you
will keep yourselves safe in God's love.

And you must show mercy to those
whose faith is wavering. Rescue others
by snatching them from the flames of
judgment. Show mercy to still others,
but do so with great caution, hating
the sins that contaminate their lives.

Now all glory to God, who is able to keep
you from falling away and will bring you
with great joy into his glorious presence
without a single fault. All glory to him who
alone is God, our Savior through Jesus
Christ our Lord. All glory, majesty, power,
and authority are his before all time, and in
the present, and beyond all time! Amen.

PART 1:

JUDE 1-4

CHAPTER 1:
CALLED TO &
KEPT FOR LOVE

There are many inspiring stories of people who have risked it all to start a church in a place that desperately needs it. These church planters work hard, and they pray even harder. Sometimes, their new and mostly unknown churches reach thousands of people, gaining a prominent place in their communities. When the rest of us hear their stories of success at conferences, we're fired up to go out and try to replicate their success.

This, however, is *not* one of those stories.

The uninspiring origin story of Madison Church begins on a Sunday in September 2014. We spent tens of thousands of dollars, invited *thousands* of people, and prayed diligently over what we believed would be a life-changing hour. It was as exciting as a relief to finally reach that point. Our small "launch team" was ready to show all their friends and family at our church's first public gathering why we all relocated to Wisconsin.

I anxiously waited outside the hotel conference center's doors that Sunday morning, envisioning myself greeting hundreds of people in our city who were spiritually curious. Their lives would never be the same again by coming to our church—they just didn't know it yet.

Of course, my life was going to change too. The church we were planting would be one of those inspirational success stories you heard about at conferences.

I waited for those crowds to arrive, but they never came. Actually, only 30 people showed up, including me. More than half of our attendees were visiting from out of town, many of whom were related to me. The only thing I thought would happen that happened was that I experienced a life change. It just wasn't the kind I hoped for. I was confident that I had wasted tens of thousands of dollars and precious time in a disaster that could be seen as far as heaven.

After a couple of long days spent feeling sorry for myself, two pastors of a nearby multisite church reached out to me. I thought they were confused and had asked the wrong pastor for coffee because they said, "We've heard really awesome things are happening at your church!"

Awesome? They were either clueless or cruel.

I agreed to meet them, though. We met the day after that initial phone call. After some small talk, they asked if our church would be interested in taking over the location they were trying to get started near us because the pastor there resigned unexpectedly. After I clarified and confirmed they were serious about their request, we agreed to take their third location and merge it with our church plant.

We met the following weekend at the community

center they'd been meeting at all summer. The monthly rate there was less than the weekly rate at the hotel. We saved a lot of money and had almost 50 people in attendance. My emotions went from the lowest of lows to the highest of highs in one week. There was renewed hope and energy in me, and I began to think it was possible I wasn't as bad at church planting as I thought I was.

Whereas a few days earlier, people had to interrogate me to get any details about how our opening went, I voluntarily called anyone who would answer their phone to tell them how our church plant more than doubled in size just one week later. I felt like the anointed and appointed one with an even more compelling success story to share at whichever conference asked me to speak first. Until the following Sunday, only four came to the lowest-attended service we've ever had in our church's history.

And just like that, I killed two churches in Madison in only three weeks.

CALLED TO FAIL?

An unfortunate part of the reality in which we live is that sometimes the things we want the most doesn't happen the way we want them to despite our best efforts. I don't have to know you well to know that something you wanted to work out didn't at some point in your life. We've all been there when we just aren't whatever, fill-in-the-blank enough.

Do you remember what you said when someone asked you, "What do you want to be when you grow up?" As kids, we'd enthusiastically answer this question. We wanted to be firefighters, rockstars, teachers, basketball players, doctors, and, sometimes, princesses. We hadn't failed enough to know that this type of question, about hopes and dreams, is deeply personal— and our answers should not be freely given out.

If you had asked me as a kid what I wanted to be when I grew up, I would've told you I would play professional football. My favorite memories as a kid were throwing a football with my dad in our backyard and watching Sunday games.

When I could finally play competitively in middle school, I worked as hard as I could to be the best football player I could be. While everyone else kept getting bigger, stronger, and faster, I didn't. In the last year I played high school football, I weighed 140 lbs. and was 5'10". Not exactly the genetic makeup of someone poised to have a stellar career in the NFL.

I was devastated. I had put so much into this hope of playing professionally one day and was faced with the reality that it most definitely wasn't going to happen at 17 years old. And while you probably didn't have a Green Bay Packers-themed bedroom growing up as I did, I'm sure you can vividly remember *that* time your aspirations didn't work out despite your best efforts. When that happens, our hearts become a little more calloused than before.

Our failures inflict emotional wounds that cause us to

settle for mediocrity, while the scars remind us why we do.

I've been told that when people get toward the end of their lives, they ask, "Did anything I do matter?" When I heard that for the first time, I noticed it's pretty much the same question as, "What do you want to be when you grow up?" Both questions are about doing something that makes being someone matter.

The questions are phrased differently based on the age and stage of life, but they're all about personal successes and failures. Most kids want to be whatever they want because they believe it will improve the world. If we get to live to an old age, we'll look back and evaluate whether we accomplished that.

At the beginning of our lives, we're asked if we want to make a difference. At the end of our lives, we ask ourselves if we did. I believe this earnest desire inside us comes from God. It gets damaged when doing *something* that matters becomes more important than being *someone* who matters. Jude confronts this thinking when he states he's writing to "all who have been called by God the Father" (**Jude 1**). What he's referring to, like his peers in the New Testament, is how God calls people into a relationship with him.

The calling Jude is writing about is not about what we do for work or have accomplished. We have been conditioned to think that calling has to do with *what* we do, but biblical calling is all about *who* we are. In the mind of God, *who* we are is vastly more important than *what* we *do*. Even if you grew up and became everything you wanted to do as a kid, you must maintain your perspective on the importance of being.

Before we can do something that makes a difference, we must accept that God has made a difference in us. We're significant beings because of God's significant doings. God made way for a relationship between him and us through the life, death, and resurrection of Jesus. God sought us out long before we could seek him. Now we can all enter the Kingdom of God because we belong there.

TO BE LOVED

This is possible because God loves us. Jude writes about a love that is quite remarkable and unlike any other (**Jude 1**). The Greek word he used is *agapaō*. In that society, *agapaō* was rarely used because it described the highest form of love. This is quite profound to take in if we can begin to grasp the impact of its meaning.

There were other words for "love" that you and I would have written on a birthday or anniversary card to tell someone important that we loved them, and it wasn't the same word we'd use to communicate the highest form of love! In stark contrast with society at that time, *agapaō* is the most used word for love in the New Testament—and it's used when writing about God's love for you and me. It's an exclusive love offered to us inclusively.

As people incapable of loving *anyone* this way, you and I can't fully understand how God can love *everyone* this way. We don't even love God the way he loves us. Our capacity to love is imperfect because we are imperfect. God's love is perfect because God is perfect and because God is love. This seems too good to be true, but it is as true as it is good.

In our incapacity to completely understand this love, it's here that we begin to realize how great God's love really is. God cannot love us more because that would mean his love for us today is lacking or incomplete. We may learn to love God more with time, but trying to earn more of God's love is a pointless pursuit. Our love for others may vary, but God's is never changing.

We can have peace and comfort that supersedes our situation and circumstances because God loves us. Much like our calling, this love for us is based on who God is and what he's done for us. God loves us regardless of how we've failed in our relationships, career, or academic pursuits. Our identities as beloved will not change because God's identity as a lover never changes.

Despite all the many reasons you have to worry about in this life, you can find peace in that God loves you all the same, yesterday, today, and forever. You can do nothing to make God love you more or less. No matter how often you've failed, you're not a failure. Similarly, no matter how much success you've had doesn't mean you're successful. Being who God calls you to be, not what you do or how well you do it, is the measure of true success in our faith.

KEPT & PROTECT

Loved is whom we're called to be, and it's where you and I are kept. Jude writes that God's love "keeps you safe in the care of Jesus Christ" (**Jude 1**). God remains in and around us, keeping us safe and secure. As with our calling and God's love, we don't have to concern ourselves about God's faithfulness.

You may have had a parent walk out of your life who should've been there for you or your closest friend left your side when you needed them the most. Two of my closest friends got divorced 10 years after "I do," despite efforts to work things out. While people will let people down regardless of intent, including you and me, God will not abandon anyone.

This doesn't mean bad things won't happen to us. We will still go through challenging times that cause long-lasting trauma and grief because we live in a world plagued by sin. God himself was subjected to the same pain and suffering we experience. Jesus felt abandoned by God on Good Friday, but Easter Sunday proved otherwise.

This also doesn't mean we don't share responsibility for our spiritual condition. If what we do or don't do has no effect on eternity, then Jude wouldn't have written a letter to people who had gotten off track. He wouldn't confront his original recipients for thinking their actions didn't matter. There would be no urgency behind his original message for them to change their ways if choices didn't make a difference to God.

God sustains us through his power, maintaining us until we've entered the life to come. It's not just a promise then and there, but here and now. We may be aware it's happening, but we might not. Sometimes it might be spiritual protection, and other times it is mental or physical. God is always at work in and around us, and how we respond matters.

RAISED TO NEW LIFE

I'm still sure that, to this day, the start of our church is one of the worst starts to a church in the history of the world. We were prayed over and funded by people who believed in God *and* us. Failing was a risk I was well aware of, but I didn't think it would happen so quickly to me. The situation facing our new church after a few short weeks was dire, but walking away wasn't going to happen. I knew we were called for and kept in love, and that gave me all I needed to go on.

Even if our endeavors in Madison failed, an idea that made my mind anxious and caused heartache, I would find rest in the knowledge of my secured identity.

During that inglorious first year, the grocery store I worked at brought in a new manager for the produce department. I could tell almost immediately that Matt was one of the friendliest and most talkative guys I knew. He was always ready to ask about anything and everything. I found time to talk to Matt about our new church. I invited him and his family to join us at our first-anniversary celebration. When the day came, I had more realistic expectations about who would show up compared to the year before.

(By that, I mean I expected *no one* to show up.)

When I saw his family getting out of their car that weekend, it gave me some joy I didn't have when we opened. What was better is that they enjoyed their time with us, connected with several others, and started participating in our Sunday gatherings and midweek groups regularly.

A few months later, Matt decided he wanted to be baptized. I learned that he grew up in and around the church but had never decided to follow Jesus for himself. We baptized Matt and three others. With each baptism, I felt myself being raised to new life.

Afterward, Matt and his wife trained to become small-group facilitators. In that role, they served as pastors and teachers for those in their group. A challenge we give all our leaders is to go out and look for ways to share their faith in our city. Based on my own experiences with Matt, this would be easy for him.

He took little time to invite a coworker from the bakery inside the same grocery store to his small group. Briana began showing up to everything we did, and God continued working in her life. She eventually indicated she had the desire to be baptized. Matt and I baptized Briana less than a year after we baptized him. She's has been on our church's staff since then, contributing in very meaningful ways.

About a year after we baptized Briana, I stood inside a

pool we bought at Target with her mom. In our church, when someone decides to get baptized, a pastor, along with the person who brought the one being baptized into the community, does the baptizing. It's been amazing to see the pictures of people who were once baptized at our church baptizing others. I realized then that we were about to baptize a third generation of believers at Madison Church. My mind went back to that first day for a moment, and I thanked God I didn't quit when times were difficult.

CALLED TO & KEPT IN LOVE

Before we can go out into the world to do anything for Jesus, we must be sure of our identity in him. That's where Jude begins this letter 2,000 years ago because he knows that without this foundation, people will be knocked down and out by those with ulterior motives.

For now, modern-day readers cannot move on without reflecting on this biblical information that leads to personal transformation. Being called to and kept in love by God is more important to our identity than our race, ethnicity, gender identity, and sexual orientation. It's more essential to our being than our political opinions and theological beliefs. Who we are isn't what we do or where we go to work on Mondays through Fridays (or Saturdays or Sundays). Those aspects of us aren't *unimportant*, but they are *less* important than being a follower of Jesus.

Once we're sure of this truth about our identities in Christ, we can be part of the solution to the many facing our world by ensuring we're not perpetuating the problem. And so, by beginning this way, Jude reinforces his ancient and modern reader's identities in God. The danger of being exploited was real then and is real today. Jude would've written a different message if this threat wasn't real. This is the subject of the following few verses and our next chapter.

CHAPTER 2:
THE LETTER JUDE DIDN'T WANT TO WRITE

Like almost everyone else in their final semester as an undergraduate student, I looked forward to putting what I learned over four years of study into practice vocationally—*and getting paid to do so!* I enthusiastically accepted an offer to become the assistant pastor at a mainline church in Southwest Missouri. My primary responsibilities were to run the student ministry at the larger campus while serving in an unofficial pastoral role for a smaller campus they had just started.

This was an exciting and unique opportunity because it combined what I was most passionate about at the time (student ministry) while providing experience in something I felt called to do later (church planting).

My first day in the office was the Monday after the 2011 Joplin tornado, an EF5-rated multi-vortex tornado that killed 158 and injured over 1,000 more. This tragic natural disaster affected *everyone* in the area. That summer, our church was a part of multiple efforts to serve our city and show them the love of God while helping them rebuild their lives. It was exhausting but always rewarding to go to work and help in such tangible ways.

The student ministry really took off over the summer, too. I developed a leadership pipeline for students, got more adults involved through volunteering, and the group went from 20 or so teenagers coming to our events to over 100 at its peak. It was fun to succeed and be recognized for doing well. I loved being a part of helping young people own their faith for the first time in their lives. It was a busy, albeit memorable and impactful, summer.

The other part of my job, the second campus, could have gone *a lot* better. It was frustrating to work so hard with little to no quantitative growth to show for it. To make matters worse, it led to a severe deterioration of my relationship with the senior pastor, who thought I was putting less effort into that part of my job.

Eventually, every text message, every phone call, and every meeting were anxiety-inducing. I became conditioned to know I could be demeaned or demoralized anytime we interacted. Throughout my short tenure, I saw him use different bullying tactics against others on staff. It's no exaggeration for me to write that he used his authority to spiritually neglect and emotionally abuse those under his leadership.

My dream job became a nightmare with each passing day until the Monday after Thanksgiving. Just a few weeks before Christmas, I was told to be out of the building by the end of the day. The senior pastor instructed me not to reach out to anyone in the church and that he drafted a letter to read to the church on my behalf the following Sunday.

The unhealthy conflict was part of the culture. I was never written up, he didn't say why I was fired, and I wasn't given a severance. My first Christmas married to Megan wouldn't be all I hoped it would be—or what anyone hopes their first Christmas married would be. Worse yet, it took us well over two years to move past the financial repercussions of being out of work for a short time.

All my enthusiasm about being in ministry took a wildly disappointing turn. I questioned my faith because how could he and I share beliefs in the same God while having drastically different ways of living it out? It would take me years to heal from the experience.

THE LETTER JUDE DIDN'T WANT TO WRITE

Like you and me, Jude knows firsthand what it's like to hope for one thing only to be disappointed by another. None of us, including the brother of Jesus, are exempt from this experience. Jude admits this very thing on the front end of his letter when he states he wanted to send them a different kind of message: "Dear friends, I had been eagerly planning to write to you about the salvation we all share. But now I find that I must write about something else..." (**Jude 3**).

Jude tells how he eagerly wanted to expound on the remarkable story of Jesus and how God changes and transforms lives. This was what he was most excited about. That message would have been familiar to the recipients. They were already followers of Jesus, and he reminded them of that in verses one and two. Still, there is something about the telling and retelling of the life, death, and resurrection of Jesus, the sinless son of God.

Jude had seen how his brother, Jesus, changed the trajectory of eternity for all who would choose to accept him. Jesus came and lived the life we should've lived, only to die the death we all deserve so that we can exist in the resurrection with him. Without the life, death, and resurrection of Jesus, the rest of us would all be damned and hell bound.

God didn't just show humanity a way to him. He made the way. God leads us to the kingdom on a path he created and traveled. The God we believe in didn't sit atop some allegorical mountain, waiting for people to figure out how to get to him. Nor did God send a prophet to say, "do this" or "don't do that." God came down from a heavenly throne, met us where we were, and offered to take our hand.

This message passed on from one generation of believers to another, was being *rewritten* rather than *retold*. Some were leading other believers *away* from the faith they had. The seriousness of that prompts the change in Jude's subject matter. What he wants from readers is far more than collaborative resistance or individual tolerance. Jude wants us to come against their lies and manipulations proactively to "defend the faith that God has entrusted once for all time to his holy people" (**Jude 3**).

To be clear, he is not instructing anyone to be a snarky keyboard warrior, calling out everything that indirectly challenges our faith or what we believe in on our social media newsfeed. That is offensive and ineffective for all involved. Jude has something better in mind for all who read. Jude gives us clear instructions on what to do, "defend the faith," but is unspecific about how we do it. He doesn't prescribe a specific model for defending the faith, just a directive.

This is an intentional choice of words because a compelling defense of our shared faith will change depending on the situation and circumstances. How Jude's original audience would've best defended their faith in the Middle East during the first century differs from how we best can wherever we find ourselves today. In Part 2, we'll discuss several ways to defend the faith in our society today.

UNNOTICED, NOT UNSEEN

It's not like Jude's friends were willfully ignorant of attempts to mislead them. That would be foolish of anyone to presume because we can all be fooled, especially when those who are misleading aren't usually apparent. Jude writes about this, "Some ungodly people have wormed their way into your churches... The condemnation of such people was recorded long ago..." (**Jude 4**).

Jude is writing about intruders and infiltrators but does not explicitly call them "false teachers." We have no reason to believe these folks had leadership positions or teaching roles. However, they certainly and evidently, had influence. The distinction is essential.

"Some ungodly people" aren't who we typically think they are.

They're usually not those we see on Netflix docuseries hoarding guns and moving their families into giant compounds on the outskirts of a town with a leader who thinks he's the Messiah. (The lunatic leader is almost always a *he*.) They can be, but they're usually less obvious and more subtle. These are the types of individuals Jude's friends were negatively affected by. They crept in unnoticed.

Jude says that what was occurring was prophesied long ago, referring to our Old Testament. We shouldn't be surprised by this happening, and it's not indicative of a group of believers doing something wrong. It was a matter of when, not if, people would infiltrate Christian communities. How we respond to these threats is imperative.

SIN ISSUES

Jude writes how some are: "saying that God's marvelous grace allows us to live immoral lives" (**Jude 4**). The message of those who have Jude worried is that we should all remain as we are because God loves everyone precisely as they are. While God's grace covers every sin we'll ever commit, we should not go on living as if what we say, do, or think doesn't matter. It's a belief that can be fatal to our relationship with God.

People have and will continue to respond to God's grace by living as they had before, with no regard for how their lives could point others to or away from God and the Christian community. But that's the fraudulent faith Jude pleads with us to reject. Professor Douglas J. Moo writes:

> "One of the points Jude is trying to get across is that truth and practice are linked together. Confessing the right things is vital if we are to live the right way. The truth of God in Christ sets people free. Surely, if we really appreciate the power of the Gospel and the blessing it brings to us, we will be more passionate in maintaining and defending it."[4]

Grace offers us a second chance at a life we don't deserve now, which means we can't continue to speak, think, and act as we did before encountering grace. God wants to save us from the demise of sin, not perpetuate its destruction. Jesus didn't come to earth to get a closer look at the damage being done. He came to us to undo the damage that's been done. In other words, Jesus loves us enough to meet us where we're at and not leave us there.

When Jude talks about living "immoral lives," he's referring to sin. While everyone has heard of sin, and most people think they know what sin is, I've found that it is commonly misunderstood. People think of sin as the things we shouldn't say, think, or do. Sin includes those, but a proper understanding is deeper than that.

Sin should also be understood in terms of the spiritual and relational "distance" it puts between us and God, us and others, and others and God. This misunderstanding about the nature of sin also takes away from the profound gift that is the Bible because it lowers the status of the biblical texts to a cosmic rulebook.

What I mean by this is that a hurtful comment isn't just wrong because it's written in the Bible. It's wrong because, in addition to that, it puts space between God and us. Sin ultimately keeps us from experiencing greater intimacy with God and each other. It's disruptive to harmonious and healthy living.

Avoiding sin isn't just about walking away from a bad thing, it's about walking toward a better one.

God calls and keeps us in his love, but that doesn't mean we can do whatever we want without consequence. That's the lie many of us have believed. There will be consequences because sin permeates our lives. Sin is not something that a few of us need to care about because it affects us all in different ways, physically and spiritually, and it has a ripple effect of damage in the world.

JESUS IS LORD

Recall that this series of verses begins with Jude expressing his desire to write another kind of letter that celebrates the life, death, and resurrection of Jesus. He was unable to because there were some who "have denied our only Master and Lord, Jesus Christ" (**Jude 4**).

What Jude wrote about in these verses, about Jesus

being our only Master and Lord, won't go unchallenged. You may object. Studies have recently shown that upwards of half of Christians in the United States think that some non-Christian faiths can lead to eternal life,[5] but that echoes some of the beliefs Jude is opposing. We must recognize that there are significant differences in the world's major religions. Some will say that "all paths lead to God," but they have not studied closely what each faith says about their path to God and what they believe about Jesus.

Islam, for example, has The Five Pillars, basic acts considered mandatory by Muslims. They say that Jesus was a prophet but is not God. People can get to paradise if they do more good things than bad throughout their lives. Hinduism, however, says that people must live a moral life to become one with Brahma. Jesus may be a god, but he's certainly not the *only* God.

Judaism and Buddhism have different beliefs about those subjects, as does Christianity, but even in their differences, each claim to offer *the* way to life after life. The common belief between Islam, Hinduism, Judaism, and Buddhism is that they teach it's up to a human effort to achieve eternal life. Our ability (or inability) to do this or that will ultimately determine our destiny. In a word, it's about doing.

This is in strong contrast to Christianity. Whereas these other faiths are about doing something, Christianity is about something done. Because Jesus came, we can know God, and eternity is a gift. Regardless of who you are or what you've done (or haven't done), Jesus offers freedom and forgiveness. And that offer isn't just good after we die, then and there.

If we understand it as Jude did, the truth about our faith and salvation is that they provide hope for the future and healing from the past.

FAITH & TRUTH

I've thought for a long time that one of the most extraordinary pieces of evidence of Jesus' deity is that his brothers call him both "Master" and "Lord." Anyone with siblings can imagine the difficulty of stating that one of them is the Messiah, let alone believing it. Jude, and his brother James, were no exception either. They weren't always believers. Check out this scene when Jesus' brothers said,

> "Why don't you leave here and go up to the Feast so your disciples can get a good look at the works you do? No one who intends to be publicly known does everything behind the scenes. If you're serious about your actions, come out in the open and show the world." *His brothers pushed him like this because they didn't believe in him.*

> **John 7:3-5 (MSG)**

Jude writes as one who knows unbelief well. His disbelief was known then and recorded for anyone with access to a Bible to read. And yet, both he and his brother had a change of heart and contributed works to the New Testament and the spread of the Gospel in the first century. So when he calls out some who deny Jesus as God, he does so as someone who has already done the same, which wasn't uncommon in their pluralistic society. The culture at the time had many gods and even considered their political leaders divine. Those whom Jude confronts were teaching about alternative paths to salvation.

Even though Jude wanted to write a different message, the letter we got is the one we've needed for two millennia. The faith of his friends and their families was under attack, although it was unbeknownst to them at the time. An assault of the kind Jude writes to prevent would negatively affect anyone's relationships with God and eternal destinies if gone unconfronted. These are problems that can still occur today.

He assures readers that the promises and pleasures of sin are temporary and do more damage than not. Our identities, as called, kept, and loved, are found in Jesus alone whose instructions are summed up simply in the most significant challenge: "Follow me." It leads us to this critical distinction: Jesus isn't *something* to be studied; he's *someone* to be followed. As we read through and study *Jude*, we must regularly consider how we can grow to be more like Jesus. If this isn't our highest priority and most important value, then discerning what is true and what isn't will be very difficult. It could also hurt the faith of those closest to us.

PART 2:

JUDE 5-16

CHAPTER 3:
UNFAITHFUL ISRAEL, IMPRISONED ANGELS, & SINFUL SODOM

The voice of God calling me to start a church sounded a lot like my college roommate, Chris, shrugging off yet another one of my rants. I spent many afternoons of my final semester in our dorm room complaining that it was too common for pastors and churches to focus on problems and people from another era. At what point in our history did we, the Christian Church, become more interested in protecting our traditions than pioneering the future?

In my view, most were more passionate about their models and methods of doing church than an entire generation of people leaving their faith. I couldn't comprehend why so much of Christianity insisted that people disown their backgrounds and experiences before coming through the doors of churches. I didn't, and still don't, think people should have to change to find Jesus in our church communities. After all, Jesus found people before they were changed.

"Start a church," Chris said, leaning closer to his computer screen. As I lay in bed that night, I could hear the voice of God saying I should do that.

And just like that, $60,000 and four years of my way through an education in psychology, only taking biblical studies courses because they were mandated as part of my college curriculum, I began to go after something new that God was doing in and through my life. I would only be able to fully pursue this later because Megan had to finish her degree first, and she was a couple of years behind me in her studies.

When that time came, we could move anywhere we wanted. We decided to stay in the Midwest after lots of prayers and an exercise we did at a church planting conference. We were instructed during a weeklong training to go back to our hotel and make a list of cities we would either like to move to or felt led to go. Super spiritual, right?

Well, it actually worked.

Megan and I made our lists in our hotel room after a day of learning and from separate beds. My list was full of places most tourists would like to visit and call home, like San Diego and Honolulu. Megan's was much more practical, closer to family and friends. Oddly enough, there was one city on both of our lists. It was a place neither of us had been to in our adult lives and one of the most post-Christian and least religious cities in the United States: Madison, Wisconsin.

We visited soon after and immediately fell in love with

Madison. We both knew with confidence that God wanted us in Madison to start the kind of church with which the city could meaningfully engage. The two of us felt more confirmation when others were shocked we'd want to move to such a "godless" place. What some intended to deter us from moving to Madison had the opposite effect.

Megan had graduated by then but had a contract with a public school district in Missouri for another year. I felt prompted to move and get to work before she could, though. Since we could not afford two places to live then, I moved to Madison, aware I could very well be homeless for a few months until she moved here after her contract and our lease expired.

With the help of a local pastor who offered a spare bed-room, I had a place to stay while I rode my bike to and from work. And, although it would be brief, everything I took to Madison was either in the backpack I wore or a duffle bag I held in my hand. It was the first of many challenging decisions I would make to be faithful.

Since I didn't know anyone from Madison, I posted about relocating on Facebook. I was looking to meet people in the city who might be open or interested in the church we were starting. That led me to my first meeting in Madison about our church with a University of Wisconsin student named Anthony.

Anthony would become the first person we baptized, and he was our first volunteer leader for the children's ministry program. He's a good friend to this day. Our lives intersected because of decisions we both made trying to pursue faithfulness many years ago.

UNFAITHFUL ISRAEL

Activating *faithfulness* in our lives becomes Jude's focus in this next set of verses. He gives three examples of God stepping in to interrupt and correct communities with varying degrees of unfaithfulness that come against his ideal for creation. Intentionally going out of the order in which these events occurred, Jude begins with the wandering generation of Israel after the Exodus:

> "So, I want to remind you, though you already know these things, that Jesus first rescued the nation of Israel from Egypt, but later he destroyed those who did not remain faithful."

> **Jude 5**

Jude emphasizes through this first example that we're all susceptible to unfaithfulness no matter where we've come from or experienced. The Israelites who escaped Egypt lived through some of the most visible examples of God's work. The generation of Israelites delivered from Egypt never experienced the Promised Land because of their unfaithfulness. It's presumably why he begins here instead of going in chronological order with the examples in this passage.

God chose Moses to lead the Israelites out of slavery in Egypt. It appears to almost not happen when they come to a dead end at the Red Sea while fleeing their

Egyptian captors. God, however, miraculously splits open the sea so the Israelites can safely walk to freedom on the other side before closing it on top of the army pursuing them.

When the people saw this from the shore on the other side, they had great faith in God and trusted in Moses. That didn't last long, though. Soon after, their faith in God and trust in Moses waned. God was faithful to the promise he made, but the community didn't remain faithful to the promise they made.

We're not talking about a lack of belief here. That community saw more signs, wonders, and miracles than most of us have today. Their flaw was their lack of trust and commitment to what they believed. They began to believe that slavery in Egypt was better than wherever God was leading them. Jude's readers would've known this story well. It's their story, how they got from *there* to *here*.

IMPRISONED ANGELS

God was trying to take the nation of Israel to freedom in the Promised Land. Their unfaithfulness was taking them back to slavery in Egypt. Unfaithfulness took them away from God's ideal for them, ultimately separating them from God. Future generations of Israel would repent and remain faithful. In Jude's second example, he writes about fallen angels who wouldn't get another opportunity to do so:

"And I remind you of the angels who did not stay within the limits of authority God gave them but left the place where they belonged. God has kept them securely chained in prisons of darkness, waiting for the great day of judgment."

Jude 6

This is one of those passages that makes Jude cryptic to a modern audience. According to the intertestamental book *1 Enoch*, some angels married humans before the flood, resulting in a race of giants. It sounds more like something of Greek mythology than anything written in biblical texts. Still, it is very briefly recorded in Genesis:

This was back in the days (and later) when there were giants in the land. The giants came from the union of the sons of God and the daughters of men. These were the mighty men of ancient lore, the famous ones.

Genesis 6:4 (MSG)

Jewish interpreters took this small passage and came up with quite the tale about these angels. First, these angels were attracted to women. At this point, the angels transformed themselves into men so they could have sex with the women. They do, and children are born as a result. This was intolerable to God, and he ensured they would never be able to do this again by imprisoning the offenders.

Faithfulness is a *choice* we make regardless of our circumstances. We've all thought from time to time that if our situation were different, then our responses to life would also be different. The angels who abandoned God proved that's not always the case.

It is a compelling illustration of the point that he was trying to make: That is, whereas the nation of Israel didn't always have proximity to God, the angels did. Nonetheless, the angels and the Israelites chose unfaithfulness and separated from God. Additionally, it builds on the previous example in that angels thought to be closest to God in actual proximity from the beginning weren't beyond the kind of unfaithfulness that leads to an abandonment of their security.

SINFUL SODOM

Unfaithfulness leads to us living outside of God's will for our lives, and the result is sin's curse. Jude writes about the pinnacle of unfaithfulness in two towns plagued by sin:

> "And don't forget Sodom and Gomorrah and their neighboring towns, which were filled with immorality and every kind of sexual perversion. Those cities were destroyed by fire and serve as a warning of the eternal fire of God's judgment."

Jude 7

Some today have made what really happened in these cities more complicated than it is. The story from the biblical texts (Genesis 19) is that angels visit a man named Lot, who was living in Sodom, late one night. A bunch of the men from the town noticed and came to his house to force themselves sexually on Lot's angelic guests.

Lot refuses to give up the angels. Instead, he offers his virgin daughters engaged to be married to the mob so they can rape the girls. The crowd didn't accept this compromise and began to break down the house door so they could enter Lot's home.

The angels protect Lot and his family for a moment and instruct him to take his family and leave the city because they've been sent to destroy the city. Lot reluctantly went along with this, getting his family out of Sodom before it was destroyed along with Gomorrah.

These towns are most often brought up in modern-day conversations about faith due to some people's opposition to gay, lesbian, and bisexual relationships. We should note the obvious: neither Genesis 19 nor Jude 7, nor any other passage in the Old or New Testaments, claims or states that same-sex relationships are why God destroyed the cities. The prophet Ezekiel elaborates the most on what the sins of Sodom were:

> "'The sin of your sister Sodom was this: She lived with her daughters in the lap of luxury— proud, gluttonous, and lazy. They ignored the oppressed and the poor. They put on airs and lived obscene lives. And you know what happened: I did away with them.'"

> **Ezekiel 16:49-50 (MSG)**

Ezekiel describes Sodom in such a way that it could be a description of most modern civilizations. He doesn't mention sexual sins as Jude does. Both describe unfaithfulness to God that brings varying degrees of death and destruction to those around them, including sexually.

ACTIVATE FAITHFULNESS

For Jude, these illustrations weren't just anomalies from a time long, long ago. They stood to show how God would eventually come against those who came against him. From the physical death of an unfaithful Israel to angels being imprisoned in darkness to the destruction of Sodom, Jude shows an escalation of joint damage when faithfulness in the community falters.

And yet, it wasn't the entire nation of Israel who didn't make it to the Promised Land, only a generation of them. Just like it wasn't all the angels who were expelled from heavenly places and bound by chains in darkness. Let's remember that not everyone was destroyed when the cities of Sodom and Gomorrah were.

We're not guilty by association, but we would do well to recognize that those who made it through were often the exceptions, not the norm. Countless others in those contexts were swept up in what the majority of those around them were doing and thus received the same fate. Whom we spend our time with is more important than we might think—especially regarding

our faith. Professor Ben Witherington III writes about
the importance of faith together regardless of the
challenges of doing so:

> "Against our modern overemphasis on indi-
> viduals being saved, we would do well to rec-
> ognize that no one is saved in or for solitude.
> A person is saved into the community of faith,
> which is not just the sum of its individual parts
> and saved to serve God."[6]

What we should do then, as communities of believers,
is come together and be faithful. James, the brother
of Jude and Jesus, tells us how: "Resist the devil, and
he will flee from you. Come close to God, and God
will come close to you" (James 4:7-8). The imagery of
this text is vivid. Simply by standing firm, which isn't
always simple to do, the one who would steal, kill, and
destroy our lives runs away from us. Moving closer to
God, the One who gives us a rich and satisfying life,
moves closer to us.

It's easier to draw near to God when things are *really*
good or *really* bad. When things are going well, we say,
"Praise God," and use #blessed for our posts. It's just
as easy to call God when things aren't going well. But
when counseling doesn't save our marriage, medicine
doesn't cure our disease, or our contingency plans fail,
we want to draw near to God out of necessity when
there are no other options left.

And yet, most of life is lived between these highs and
lows. Milestones are fun to celebrate, but life takes
place between them. Most of us need to get better at

connecting with God in the mundane of life. As a matter of fact, when we don't feel like we need to draw nearer to God is when we need to draw nearer to him the most. Connecting with God isn't something we do for an hour once or twice a week. It's something that should occur regularly in our lives. Every decision we make is a decision to move closer to, or further from, God.

God needs to be first in our life. If God isn't first, praying, reading the Bible, going to church, or whatever other spiritual disciplines we do are just religious *obligations*. When I'm first in my life, I read the Bible to get advice or not feel guilty. If your life is about you, praying is about something you want or need. When faith is catered and tailored to our personal preferences so that we can remain first in our lives, it's not sustainable.

Genuine faith requires God to be first. When God is, praying, reading the Bible, or going to church isn't just about something I need or want... It's about connecting with our Maker. In our pursuit to become like Jesus, we begin by practicing faithfulness.

WHEN JESUS WAS MOST LIKE US

There's a story we tell a lot around Easter Sunday, but I think it's one we should tell more often. It's about when I believe that Jesus was most like you and me. The night that Jesus was betrayed, a day before his horrible death, he was wildly aware of what was about to happen. It's not like life had always been easy for Jesus. He faced great temptations and trials at different points throughout his life, as all of us have, but this was going to be the most challenging time of his life. As he reflects on the betrayal and his subsequent death, he prays:

> "Father, remove this cup from me. But please, not what I want. What do you want?" At once an angel from heaven was at his side, strengthening him. He prayed all the harder. Sweat, wrung from him like drops of blood, poured off his face.

Luke 22:42-44 (MSG)

Like most of us, when faced with something excruciating, Jesus asks God to let him skip it. He asks for a way out or around it. We can relate to this. We'd instead not go through the bad parts of life. And yet, as the story goes, God doesn't answer Jesus' prayer. At this point, how we react and how Jesus responds differs drastically. When faced with a great challenge, Jesus draws closer to God. He remains faithful. We try to take control of our lives instead. We may even pray that God's will be done in our lives, but we're really praying for God's will to be our will. When it's not, we become unfaithful. Jude's plea is that we submit to God's authority, even when it's hard to do so.

CHAPTER 4:
TESTAMENT OF MOSES

The first few times I read through *Jude* in preparation for the study we did at our church, my mind kept thinking about the different and well-known religious cults and their leaders. These stories of mass manipulation, the subjects of countless docuseries and fictionalized films on our favorite streaming channels must have been whom Jude intended to warn us about.

Right?

To those on the inside of a cult, they see themselves as living a more pure and disciplined life than the rest of society. For those of us on the outside, we've seen how these extreme religious movements become dangerous to all associated. How do so many people get lured into these situations?

I'm not an expert on this topic, but there is a pattern in which a manipulative leader slowly wins over and preys on people over time. This is how normal, intelligent folks get sucked in. Although rare, some can escape after years of this kind of captivity. They've written books and done TV interviews about what they experienced and how they got out. Most others are not as fortunate.

Even though the movements begin with one leader, the belief system takes a deep hold on others with influence. Now it's not only the singular leader using their influence to manipulate people. It's community-wide. This is no more evident than in groups where parents allow their children to be severely beaten, sexually assaulted, and sometimes even killed. This is what happened in Guyana in 1978.

In one of the most extreme cult activities in recent history, 900 children and adults died in a mass murder and mass suicide, drinking a flavored drink mixed with cyanide at People Temple in Jonestown. A man named Jim Jones started Peoples Temple after leaving a job at a Methodist Church in Indiana because they wouldn't allow him to integrate students of other races into their youth ministry. What began as a step in the right direction by confronting racism ended with nearly a thousand people losing their lives.

There are many, many other cults to choose from. These tragic stories capture our attention because the narratives seem implausible and unbelievable. While *Jude* certainly applies to these extreme sects, it's not limited to them. If it were, his letter would be irrelevant to most people in human history. It's not for someone else, somewhere else. We must acknowledge this while reading the text, or we'll miss God's intended impact on us through it.

If ever there was a time to talk about the extremism of those movements and their leaders, it would be now. They reveal a possible, albeit unlikely, worst-case scenario of what happens once communities of faith beliefs on the supernatural and human authority get watered down.

DREAMING OF AUTHORITY

Jude warns of some who "claim authority from their dreams" and that it leads to "immoral living" (**Jude 8**). According to Jude, by the time someone completely rejects human authority, they've already dismissed divine authority. Those who don't submit to the leadership of any person won't submit to God's, either. It's not something that *might* happen later, or that is going to happen at another time. It's something that is *already* happening.

Recall how the people of Israel, the angels, and the towns of Sodom and Gomorrah began living immorally after they defied God's authority. Those were ancient examples to the original readers, and Jude transitions to the present. What happened thousands of years before their time is happening again in front of them.

Some of those Jude writes about here claimed to receive divine revelations through their dreams. They said that these unverifiable visions "from God" gave them authority over others and allowed them to live without any authority from others. Jude says they're actually "defying authority" (**Jude 8**).

Jude isn't advocating for some spiritual hierarchy, as if our faith should be treated as a Fortune 500 Company with God as CEO and trickling downwards to different levels of spiritual management. Putting ourselves under one's authority is about *humility*, not a form of spiritual slavery. It's a willing and conscious choice we make, giving someone else the permission and encouragement to speak freely in our lives—even when it hurts our feelings or makes us mad.

WHEN JUDE WOULD HAVE WARNED *YOU* ABOUT *ME*

About a year after we moved to Madison, another family came to take over a campus ministry at the University of Wisconsin. We were both credentialed ministers through the same denomination and tried to work together when possible. My hope and belief were that both our ministries would go further faster through collaboration with one another.

Our church would join many others, supporting them through some finances, and he would speak at our church every few months. He and his wife would also play and sing in our band each month. We didn't meet outside church settings very often, but the last time we did was memorable.

As we sat down after ordering our coffees, he confronted me before saying anything else: "Do you drink alcohol?" He wasn't asking out of curiosity. Someone had told him, hoping to get me in trouble with our leadership. Consuming alcohol was against the denomination's rules for those of us with ministerial credentials.

I did have a beer from time to time but did not think it was a big deal. He did and told me I could confess on my own or he would report me. This was about something other than helping me—it was to hurt me. I decided not to acknowledge my wrongdoing and informed him of that. He immediately stopped playing in our band and speaking at our church.

I thought it was the end of the conflict. It wasn't.

He emailed our district superintendent, who called a meeting with me and other leaders in the district. I didn't know the purpose of getting together until I got there because I didn't yet know an email had been sent about the conversation I had over coffee months earlier. The tone of the meeting was hostile, with the superintendent stating he wanted to terminate me from my position as the pastor of our church, but knew he could not.

Later, I was instructed to come to a meeting of the district's entire leadership to discuss whether I could keep my ministerial credentials. Since the superintendent couldn't remove me from the church I started, this was his next attempt to rid our network of me. I was unprepared for the last meeting, but I would be ready to fight this time.

I tried to minimize my offense while attacking his credibility as a leader. He fought back, calling for the board to vote to remove my credentials. The room was tense during and after our exchange. Everyone except a pastor named John seemed in disarray and on edge. From across the room, I could see John tearing up. It made me want to cry despite how furious I was then.

John spoke life into my life at that moment, processing aloud how he felt he needed to protect me. He offered to meet with me regularly. The board didn't vote to remove my credentials if I met with John, which I gladly did.

Accountability became a good thing for me that day. None of us are perfect people, but the right people will help you be better. Meeting with John was some of the most impactful time I've spent in ministry. At the end of it, I met with our district superintendent. I apologized for breaking our rules regarding alcohol consumption and for being so hostile at our meeting.

TESTAMENT OF MOSES

Jude says the same people who reject authority also "scoff at supernatural beings" (**Jude 8**). Some of Jude's recipients have become so arrogant and consider themselves too intelligent to believe in such "primitive" ideas as angels and demons. Jude, however, draws a *different* conclusion based on the *same* information. He does not believe that someone who rejects belief in the supernatural is more intellectual than one who does. On the contrary, those who don't believe in the spiritual are ignorant of the workings of things unseen and supernatural.

Jude moves into a story that most of us reading don't know is a scene derived from the *Testament of Moses*. Only one incomplete manuscript of the *Testament of Moses* has ever been found. About half of it, including its ending, needs to be recovered. What Jude references here is thought to be in the portion that has never been found. Jude writes:

> "But even Michael, one of the mightiest of the angels, did not dare accuse the devil of blasphemy but simply said, 'The Lord rebuke you!' (This took place when Michael was arguing with the devil about Moses' body)."

Jude 9

While it would've been a story familiar to his original audience, it's one of the stories Jude tells that confuses modern readers. Jewish traditions about Moses' death were varied. In a document that does not exist today, it's thought to contain a farewell from Moses to Joshua before Moses' death and Joshua's induction as Israel's new leader.

The story goes something like this: Moses died, and God sent the archangel Michael to bury him. Michael is confronted by the devil, who says Moses belongs to him since Moses murdered some Egyptians early on in his life. The devil commonly acted as an accuser in Old Testament and Jewish literature.

Instead of Michael taking a defensive or offensive posture, he rebukes the accuser. *Moses was a murderer.* There was no point for Michael in disputing that. Moses wouldn't have denied that. Michael doesn't challenge the devil's accusations but defers the issue to the supreme judge: God.

The bottom line for Jude in this reference is that if even

a mighty angel waited for judgment from God, how much more should help people? If we assume the role of one who can make judgments, we put ourselves in a position to receive God's judgment.

To be human is to want to be completely autonomous and hence, unaccountable for what they say and do. This was no different 2,000 years ago. Jude shows that *not even the angels*, including the archangel Michael, *are entirely autonomous*. In this way, those Jude warns read that some really need help understanding even the basics of what they claim to be experts in. They attempted to separate the soul from the body, hoping that what happened to one wouldn't affect the other.

Again, Jude concludes differently. Those misleading some were *carnal* and unreasoning, whereas Michael, an angel, was wholly spiritual and yet rational. Some thought of themselves as so spiritual that the physical didn't matter, which hurt their minds, bodies, and spirits.

Some asserted that they had spiritual insights and divine authority, but Jude asserts they're more like animals without a conscience. "These people scoff at things they do not understand. Like unthinking animals, they do whatever their instincts tell them, and so they bring about their own destruction" (**Jude 10**).

Jude is heavy-handed in his critique of those who don't believe in the supernatural. What is substantial about this line is that he now speaks as one with a prophetic consciousness. Like the prophets of the Old Testament, he makes a prophetic judgment announcement.

Jude is no longer citing the prophets.

He's speaking as one of them.

Much like the generation of Israel who never made it to the Promised Land, the angels who became imprisoned in darkness for eternity, and the cities surrounding Sodom that were burned down, those who act unaccountably are bringing destruction on themselves. Because there is no accountability, there is no humility. There is no one they would be willing to receive correction from. It's not that they couldn't, but they ignored it. Professor Andrew M. Mbuvi writes:

> "The infiltrators are described as ignorant of the working of the Christian God, which results in their blaspheming. It is not that they do not have the capacity to comprehend or understand, rather they deliberately refuse to accept the nature of the Christian faith, and as a result of this failure, their actions lead them to do things that are destructive to the faith and ultimately to themselves."[7]

This isn't a "slippery slope" argument by Jude, speculating that a tiny step in the wrong direction will lead to some eternal damnation. Instead of writing about several historical examples already, Jude shows that this is what has happened and what will happen again if the pattern isn't disrupted. There's no speculation here because it's already occurred several times and places before. What we think and know about our spirituality and what we do physically directly affects others.

It's also still possible to make changes. If it were too late for Jude's original audience, then he wouldn't have written them this warning. If you're reading this, you're alive, and there's still time to turn things around, no matter how significantly you messed up or gone off track. This goes back to our identities as those called to and kept for love.

LOSING MY RELIGION

What I regret the most about the situation I wrote about earlier was how I let two guys, neither of whom are in their positions anymore, influence so much how I felt and what I did more than anyone else did at the time, including Jesus. Even toward the end, I wasn't who I should've been in my attitude.

I came up short as a follower of Jesus in so many ways during the ordeal, and John helped me see that. I made mistakes, as we all do, but it took me a long time to own up to that. Even if I told the truth about the rules I broke, I still broke the rules I agreed to follow. What's worse is how I handled myself in the fallout. My folly wasn't that I didn't know enough about Jesus' teachings. It was that I needed to follow them better.

Biblical literacy isn't tantamount to spiritual maturity. The thing keeping most of us from growing in our faith isn't more information. It's life transformation—which occurs as we follow Jesus. Luke records Jesus as telling crowds of people what it means to really follow him.

"If any of you wants to be my follower, you must give up your own way, take up your cross daily, and follow me. If you try to hang on to your life, you will lose it. But if you give up your life for my sake, you will save it. And what do you benefit if you gain the whole world but are yourself lost or destroyed?"

Luke 9:23-25

In his own words, Jesus states that for us to follow him, it's about something we do, not just something we believe. Indeed, what we think impacts what we do, but our spiritual maturity isn't measured by what we know. Too many of us today learn more about the Bible than we can put into practice. (And rest assured, there will not be a test on your theological and biblical proficiency administered after you die to determine where you'll spend eternity!)

The problem isn't in *knowing* what we should do. It's whether we're *doing* it. This makes humility essential to our faith. As we walk in the footsteps of Jesus, we learn to let go of parts of our lives we didn't know existed. When people talk to me about how their faith has stagnated, they almost invariably believe the solution involves learning new information about ancient cultures or original languages. That's seldom the solution because it has nothing to do with the problem.

ACTIVATE HUMILITY

After that season of being in trouble, meeting with

John, and learning to develop humility through accountability, I wanted to make sure it would be something practiced in our church community. So, to be a volunteer leader, serve on a board, or be on staff, we require leaders to think "we before me."

The idea behind "we before me" is humility. *Humility requires accountability.* We all need to be humble enough to find other believers who will keep us accountable and hold us responsible. Those who will lovingly call us out if we don't do what we know we ought to do. When this happens the right way, we are loved and accepted, no matter our shortcomings.

Accountability isn't about being perfect or catching someone in the act of imperfection. It's about helping someone become a better version of themselves, the kind of person God intended them to become. We can't do this alone. We must be willing to learn from others who can see our shortcomings in a way that we're unable to.

Humility is something that we must develop with the help of others. We must submit every aspect of our lives to Jesus' commands, no matter how uncomfortable that might make us feel. We need people further down on their journey of faith than us. This helps us remain faithful. If we don't have people in our lives who partner with us in this way, then we're more likely to have a substantial gap between what we claim to believe and how we live.

CHAPTER 5:
CAIN'S ENVY, BALAAM'S GREED, & KORAH'S REBELLION

Megan and I learned early on in our marriage the importance of giving back to God our first and our best because, at first, we didn't. We both had our own cars and car loans to go with them. I couldn't afford an engagement ring I thought would be good enough to express my love for her, so I financed that ring with a credit card. We also financed our wedding ceremony and honeymoon on a private loan.

I rationalized that we'd *ideally* only get married once, so I justified going big.

After we returned from the honeymoon and moved into our first place together, we got another credit card and bought some furniture. With my new, high-paying job, we could quickly pay all these things back in no time. We didn't think anything of it simply because we didn't know what we didn't know.

Just writing out all that debt makes me anxious today!

The sudden loss of my job, along with our debt, led to a very stressful and dark time in both our lives. We had the "normal" problems first-year married couples had, but the financial pressures took everything to the next level. I applied for about 10 jobs a day for a couple of months but have not had any leads or job offers.

I couldn't even pass Walmart's pre-screening questionnaire to apply for a job.

Megan kept taking undergraduate courses while working part-time as an administrative assistant at the university. Our income was around $1,000 a month, depending on how many hours she worked. The late payments and fees began to build up while our credit scores were demolished. We paid for groceries with food stamps. We moved into low-income housing, which still took half of Megan's monthly earnings.

A hot date, which we insisted on doing so that we'd have something to look forward to, was a one-dollar movie at a video store and a five-dollar pizza, using a $20 bill my father-in-law, Ray, would send us in the mail. The rest would put gas in our car. This is how we "lived" for over a year.

We were so desperate with our finances that we decided to go all in with them and God. It's not like we didn't know we were supposed to give back in some capacity to the local church. I *incorrectly* rationalized and spiritualized that doing such a thing at that time would be irresponsible.

We chose to start giving to the local church even

though we couldn't afford all the bills we had as it was. At our lowest point, I did something I've always been pretty good at: I complained to God. I prayed, "God, if we give faithfully, as you command, and we can't afford to pay our rent and end up homeless, it's on you, not me."

DOUBLE BLESSING

That desperate prayer would change our lives, along with our commitment to give our first and best back to God. I know I shouldn't have been surprised, but I was surprised that God didn't let us down. He gave us more than we hoped. Only a month after we decided to give a percentage of our income back to our local church, I found out that a grocery store where I worked as a teenager opened a location on the other side of town.

I hoped to get an interview because of my experience with them, and I did. I shouldn't have though. There was a corporate policy I didn't know about that said they had to take transfers from other stores if the employee was in good standing with the company. The human resources manager *thought* I was transferring, so I got an interview.

God seemed to work in a clerical error to get me an interview which led to a job offer. They hired me with a part-time schedule at nine dollars an hour, but that was enough to double our monthly income.

I continued to work and earn. With some unexplainable provisions, Megan and I paid off most of our debt before moving to Madison. God did more than provide for us. He helped us find financial freedom and peace. It all started when we decided to use the money how God desired us to.

The blessings didn't stop there. To my surprise, this same grocery store that I worked at as an early teen-ager and was working at now because of a logistical error was opening a new store within a mile of where we were moving to in Southwest Madison. That time I transferred!

It's the only time I was offered a job without apply-ing for it first! And within a month of working in cus-tomer service, I was asked to be the manager of the in-store Starbucks. I gladly accepted, and our house-hold income again doubled. Those paychecks paid for supplies and materials our new church needed while providing for our family.

(Remember, I couldn't even apply for a job at Walmart because I couldn't pass their online screener.)

Megan and I continued to give, and the Starbucks I managed quickly became one of the most profit-able for its size in the region. We knew we could never go back to how we lived before. Everything we have belongs to God, and we give back at least a tenth of it to the local church.

In doing this, we may temporarily have less payday, but God is for us. And when I took a substantial pay cut to work full-time at the church we started, we increased the percentage of our giving. No financial advisor in the world would suggest this, but it's what we did. God was faithful. Our church and family grew in every category we counted.

CAIN'S ENVY

One of the first areas of our lives that we get off track with God is our finances. We know who we are, and that we're supposed to be faithful, but without accountability, money can subtly become our idol. Jude transitions to this precise point in verse 11 with three examples of Old Testament men who did just that. The first of Jude's examples is Cain, the son of Adam and Eve: "For they follow in the footsteps of Cain, who killed his brother" (**Jude 11**).

The writer of Genesis tells us that Cain grew up and farmed. The reason many of us know about Cain is because of what begins to transpire here:

> "Time passed. Cain brought an offering to God from the produce of his farm. Abel also brought an offering, but from the firstborn animals of his herd, choice cuts of meat. God liked Abel and his offering, but Cain and his offering didn't get his approval. Cain lost his temper and went into a sulk."

> **Genesis 4:3-5 (MSG)**

We read that what Abel offered to God was an abundant variety of choice meats—something that Abel no doubt would've instead eaten than burned up. Cain, however, didn't bring the best he had, so God didn't accept it. This infuriates Cain, and God takes notice:

> "God spoke to Cain: 'Why this tantrum? Why the
> sulking? If you do well, won't you be accepted?
> And if you don't do well, sin is lying in wait for
> you, ready to pounce; it's out to get you, you've
> got to master it.'"

Genesis 4:6-7 (MSG)

God confronts Cain about his envy and assures him that he will be accepted if he does what he knows is right. Yet, instead of having a change of heart, Cain allows envy to overtake him and kills his younger brother. Abel's murder both angers and saddens God. He banishes Cain and removes him from his presence. And yet, God graciously offers Cain lifelong protection even during his punishment.

God's mercy for Cain is only rivaled by his desire for Abel's justice.

This story is about an internal struggle between good and evil in which evil overcame Cain. This sinful act doesn't just impact Cain; it ends Abel's life. That's Jude's point for his audience. He observes that envy, like Cain's, is one of the issues within the community he writes to. To "follow in the footsteps" refers to a life-style. Jude is not talking about a few bad decisions over a long period. He's talking about *envy* being a primary aspect of their identities.

Envy is a feeling of discontentment over someone else's possessions or qualities. It always leads to resentment.

We all feel envious at different times, but Jude warns us not to ignore it. We might assume that Cain purposely withheld his best from God, but this may not be true. It could've simply been a lack of intentionality on Cain's part, or he might've been having a tough season. Cain's quality might not have been as good as Abel's, so he tried to make up for it in the quantity he had, which meant giving less to God.

We may not know precisely where Cain's head or heart was, but we certainly know where they were not. The uncomfortable truth for us today is that we may be more like Cain than we'd care to admit, even if it's not intentional.

We had an unexpected expense, are really stressed out, or had a busy week. You and I can easily become people who frequently give God a few shoddy efforts of us, like Cain, instead of consistently offering an abundant variety, like Abel. This leads to us being mad at others when God favors them, like Cain got angry at Abel when God accepted him. While we may not take others' lives through violence as Cain did, we take people's lives through our thoughtless words about and passive-aggressive actions toward them.

We've all been guilty of this at one time or another. For some of us, this is who we are all the time. We're always upset with people. We never give God our best. This isn't just unhealthy for us. As Jude's warning goes, it affects the relationships those around us have with God and each other. God wants our faith to supersede the situations and circumstances we find ourselves in. If we don't, our envy will evolve into something worse.

BALAAM'S GREED

Jude takes us from Cain's envy to the blatant greed seen in a man named Balaam. This may mean that Jude believes envy precedes greed as Balaam is historically known for his greed: "Like Balaam, they deceive people for money" (**Jude 11**).

There are some conflicting narratives about Balaam. The people who wrote and talked about Balaam are seemingly torn about the content of his character. But for Jude and his readers, Balaam was a sellout who offered prophecies for pay and helped lead Israel into immorality and idolatry. Continuing with Jude's focus in this passage, being greedy isn't just negatively impacting us.

People in our communities will suffer when we're stingy. Our lack of generosity, directly and indirectly, leads people away from the faith. People will be turned off by our hypocrisy in claiming to be people of a God who loves so much that he gives so much when we love a little and provide even less. When we are unaccountably envious, something that is primarily *cognitive*, we become uncontrollably greedy, which is inherently *behavioral*.

KORAH'S REBELLION

Learning to think and act how God wants us to with our personal finances is difficult, but doing more of the same things we've done will get us more of the same things we've always gotten. If we want different ends, we must have other means. As he did in verses 5-7, Jude does not follow a chronological order in his unpacking. He works backward from Balaam to Korah. If envy leads to greed, then Jude implies that greed leads to division.

In Jude's final comparison, he writes: "And like Korah, they perish in their rebellion" (**Jude 11**). Korah is less known than Cain or Balaam to many of us. We read about the beginnings of Korah's rebellion against Moses and God while the Israelites are wandering in the wilderness in Numbers:

> "Getting on his high horse one day, Korah son of Izhar, the son of Kohath, the son of Levi, along with a few Reubenites—Dathan and Abiram sons of Eliab, and On son of Peleth—rebelled against Moses. He had with him 250 leaders of the congregation of Israel, prominent men with positions in the Council. They came as a group and confronted Moses and Aaron, saying, 'You've overstepped yourself. This entire community is holy, and God is in their midst. So why do you act like you're running the whole show?'"

Numbers 16:1-3 (MSG)

Korah clearly had some influence as he organized a couple of hundred others to rebel against the leadership of Moses. Israel had been lost for some time in history, so it's easy to imagine the frustration Korah and his followers had before confronting Moses.

God had done amazing things to get these people

out of Egypt. There were plagues so that those who enslaved them would release them, the sea parted so that they could cross before swallowing up their enemies, and food fell out of the sky when they were hungry (just to name a few). It's reasonable that Korah believed Moses' leadership was the problem and the reason why they weren't already at the Promised Land.

Moses and Korah have a long verbal exchange, ending with the ground opening up and killing Korah and his followers.

Cain's envy got him banished.

Balaam's greed got him imprisoned.

Korah's division resulted in his death.

Now, the ground isn't going to open and take divisive people anymore. However, the point still remains: division leads to all sorts of death. And it usually begins with what seems like harmless envy.

A TALE OF TWO MASTERS

It's unlikely that you and I are more like this Old Testament trio than when it comes to our own money. While none of us think we're rich, we all believe we're generous. The reality is that there is some truth in both. This makes sense because most of us work hard for many hours a week, only to barely make ends meet. We often feel like we need *more* to be generous.

Additionally, in our consumerist society, we're constantly told and sold that we're not enough because we don't have enough. Ads for just about every product in the world we can buy are on the TV, on our social media platforms, and inside the venues hosting our favorite musical artists and sports teams.

So, when we have a little extra cash, we've already got our eyes on a newer car, a bigger house, or a better iPhone. We try to catch up on past due bills or finally replace that broken appliance in our home. And it's just for a moment when the item is ordered and taken off our Amazon wish list that we forget how much we envy those who have more.

When the thrill of the buy is over, we tell ourselves that we'll give away more when we make more—as if something as simple as a raise or promotion at work could transform our hearts more than God's love can. But being generous is not an issue of how much (or little) we have.

Practicing generosity comes down to whether we trust in God with whatever we have. It's a heart, not money, issue. God has promised to provide us with everything we need. We don't feel like we have enough, even though we serve the God of everything. Jesus warns us:

> "You can't worship two gods at once. Loving one God, you'll end up hating the other. Adoration of one feeds contempt for the other. You can't worship God and Money both."

Matthew 6:24 (MSG)

It was not unintentional that when discussing having *undivided* loyalty, Jesus brought up finances. Money has been, and always will be, what divides our loyalties. People go to jail for stealing from others, couples divorce over financial issues, and many have walked away from their church community over teachings on money and possessions. Both Jude and Jesus' warning is plain: If we *love* money, we will end up hating God; or our adoration for gold will feed contempt toward God.

There is a direct correlation between how we think about money and how we think about God. But worse, our choice regarding this matter will impact others just as the choices of Cain, Balaam, Korah, and those in Jude's original audience impacted *others*.

ACTIVATE GENEROSITY

Giving God the rest of whatever is leftover of our time, energy, and money for the week, month, or year is not a good way to live. I certainly did for a while. That contrasts with our heavenly father, who gives us his best first. In a passage from the New Testament that often shows up on a poster board at college football games, we read: "For this is how God loved the world: *He gave...*" (John 3:16).

Generosity, according to biblical texts, is love in action.

Before we ever took our first breath or gave away our first dollar, God showed great love for us with the most generous act in human history. There are several ways for us to heed Jude's warning today. Start giving something to your local church, regularly. This step is tricky because it means saying no to something, but people quickly find that they've said yes to something better.

Stay away from getting stuck there, though. Generosity, like every other aspect of our lives, is an area we should grow in. In the Old Testament, people brought 10% of their earnings to God through the Temple, and in the New Testament, we see people giving upwards to 100% through the Early Church.

There are countless stories of people we know personally, who have taken this step of faith, including ourselves, and have seen God do just as he promised he would. With accountability in our lives, we can be faithful when it comes to giving. This would otherwise be a private matter that easily erodes our faith. As we'll see next, what some try to keep private eventually comes out for all to see—as do their consequences.

CHAPTER 6:
SHAMELESS SHEPHERDS, WANDERING STARS, ETC.

It was Friday, March 13, 2020, and I was told over the phone that our church would not be able to meet in the neighborhood center on Sunday because of precautions they were taking for the coronavirus. The person I talked with said she hoped we would be back in May. This was a devastating, unexpected announcement. Easter Sunday was less than a month away, so we couldn't gather. Like most churches, we had plans to host a fun community event.

I definitely didn't understand the severity of the new virus at the time. I knew it wasn't *good*, but I also didn't know how *bad* it was. We wouldn't be back for an in-person gathering in 2020 on Madison's west side.

After the initial shock wore off over the weekend, I acted fast to mobilize a small team from our church to serve those in our city who would be most affected by the shutdowns. Some of our leaders and I assembled a few hundred "Covid Kits." The hoarding had already begun, but we could purchase canned goods, cleaning supplies, and toilet paper. We placed the items into shopping bags and delivered them to several folks in our neighborhood's low-income housing units.

While we were busy doing that, scientists and researchers worldwide were already working toward a vaccine, doctors everywhere tried hard to save lives, and governments put together plans to keep their communities safe with mask mandates and stay-at-home orders. Everyone had a part to play in the recovery from the pandemic because everyone was affected by it.

It's been a global catastrophe that's lasted well over two years at the time I'm writing this, resulting in the death of millions worldwide. None of us have experienced this kind of crisis over that same length of time before.

We can't even see what's causing this pain and suffering with our eyes. It takes a trained professional with the right equipment in a laboratory to see and study the virus and its variants. Those experts relay information to the public to protect ourselves and those around us.

Similarly, Jude knows what he is looking at and is sharing the information so readers can protect themselves and those around them from those who can be as deadly to the soul as the coronavirus is to the body. Those who "wormed" their way into the body of believers Jude loves came in quietly, infected people quickly, and became an issue everyone had to deal with. It becomes apparent in this section of verses that there were even variants of them, as not all of them went about their manipulations the same way.

SHIPWRECKED & SHAMELESS

Jude leans into several metaphors from nature at this point, transitioning from the previous examples of events and people from the Old Testament. These are those who claimed and even appeared to be faithful, humble, and generous, but were not. And yet, it appeared in different ways. Jude writes that some "are like dangerous reefs that can shipwreck you" (**Jude 12**).

The ancient concept Jude is working with here is like a modern idiom that most of us today are familiar with: the tip of the iceberg. This phrase warns that something may be far more complex beneath the surface than what is easily seen from the surface. We've heard this before because of the iceberg that sank the Titanic.

On April 14, 1912, the navigators aboard the Titanic saw what appeared to be a small iceberg from a distance. Still, they couldn't see that upwards to 90% of the iceberg's mass was below the water. They only saw "the tip of the iceberg," and over 1,500 people died. Just as a primarily unseen iceberg can sink a massive ship made of steel, the hidden rocks near the shore Jude alludes to could cause a deadly shipwreck.

The danger of reefs under the water is only readily seen once one is too close to do anything except try to minimize the damage and survive. Jude implores us to be aware of what is unseen, and not in an exclusively spiritual sense either. Jude goes on the offense, "They are like shameless shepherds who care only about themselves" (**Jude 12**).

Shepherds were, by profession, responsible for protecting a flock of sheep from several potential dangers, like getting lost, falling off a cliff, or being eaten by a predator. Jude writes that those we should watch out for may act as if they care for us but are the real danger to our survival.

The spiritual imposters of Jude's time were leveraging their influence to benefit themselves at the cost of the common good. They were manipulative. It wasn't just a rebellion against God and the community but exploitation. They were as dangerous to them as underwater rocks are to ships because they discreetly sought to benefit themselves at the expense of the greater community.

DROUGHTS & FAMINES

Jude says we are to watch out for people who "are like clouds blowing over the land without giving any rain" (**Jude 12**). We may see some coming while not realizing the danger that follows because they present themselves as something different than they are.

The ancient readers lived in an arid climate, so clouds promised the rain they needed to create and sustain life in their region. This was long before grocery stores, greenhouses, artificial irrigation systems, and a system to transport food from all over the world to their local community. A drought in that first-century era was the difference between life and death for millions of people.

If clouds formed, everyone would anticipate a much-needed rain and everything that it would bring necessary for life. When it didn't rain, people were more than a little disappointed. They were worried about their survival. What would they eat months later when their crops died? How would they make money when they had nothing to sell? Were their families going to starve to death?

Jude is talking about the empty promises of individuals that bring no benefit to the community. Such people are like clouds that don't provide rain for the ground and instead block out the sun. Some among us may look good and be influential, but it's all an appearance. What they do is leave behind something less than nothing. Jude further emphasizes this, "They are like trees in autumn that are doubly dead, for they bear no fruit and have been pulled up by the roots" (**Jude 12**).

Like clouds that we expect to bring rain to create life, certain trees are expected to bring something to sustain life. Cloudy days go quickly, but trees take years to grow before they produce fruit. If they didn't create, they were pulled up by the roots. People would then plant something in its place that would produce something beneficial to them. They didn't just let an un-producing tree take up space, time, and other resources.

Whether someone is like a cloud, coming and going quickly, or a tree, around for a while, they both appear to bring something that would create and sustain life but don't. Such people are unreliable and unstable.

CONTAMINATED

Jude breaks from the previous metaphors with one about splashing waves of polluted water: "They are like wild waves of the sea, churning up the foam of their shameful deeds" (**Jude 13**).

Clouds that don't bring rain and trees without fruit represent those who produce nothing despite promising something. Unseen reefs are like others that quietly go about causing trouble. Splashing waves, however, look harmless enough as they wash up the pollution. In this analogy, Jude is talking about those who don't seem harmful but are deadly.

It's estimated that at least 2 billion people worldwide drink water contaminated with feces. Polluted water transmits many different types of diseases, resulting in the death of hundreds of thousands of people each year. The issue is sometimes that there needs to be access to clean water. Other times, people can't see the contaminants in the water they're drinking.

It's not just a health issue, either. Dirty water contributes negatively to education, time, and women's rights. Not having access to clean water affects the body, mind, and spirit. It's a holistic issue, as is Jude's warning against those who are like contaminated water. They may appear to be something we're familiar with, but they bring toxins.

We must be aware and cautious of people in our lives whose trouble seems to follow. They bring out the worst in others and in every situation. This isn't pessimism or a negative mindset. It's actual destruction. They don't appear alarming at first but are as polluted as the foaming sea, leaving their filth on whatever they encounter.

WANDERING STARS

Jude looks to the night sky to conclude this segment of metaphors: "They are like wandering stars, doomed forever to blackest darkness" (**Jude 13**). He references *1 Enoch* again, returning to the fallen angels' story in this analogy of wandering stars. Enoch writes about these fallen angels as wandering stars, and Jude points out that both are forever bound to darkness.

Since stars don't move in space without reason or purpose, Jude's analogy is that whatever type of analogy someone fits into, they are lost and exist without a purpose. Furthermore, regardless of which type of person they are—or we are—fate is the same, and it's not the promise of life and eternity Jesus offers.

All the comparisons promise one thing but do not deliver on them. Most of the analogies Jude used 2,000 years ago are relevant and understandable today. They're problems that continue to plague us. It makes for an adequate warning. Regardless of what "variant" of religious fraud one is, they don't do what they've been created to do. Lecturer Richard Bauckham, a foremost expert on *Jude*, writes about Jude's effective use of analogy in this section,

"Much of the impact of this passage derives from its imaginative force. Many of Jude's readers no doubt found the false teachers impressive and persuasive, and part of Jude's task must be to shift their whole imaginative perception of the false teachers and show the false teachers in a wholly different light. With this aim he provides a series of imaginatively powerful images which will influence the range of mental associations with which his readers perceive the false teachers."[8]

A BETTER WAY

Does all of this mean we should attempt to be perfectionists? Not at all. That would be an endless endeavor. Jude began his letter by talking about God's love for us and what Jesus had already accomplished for every person who lived. Jude knew well enough that the problem within the faith community wasn't that people weren't perfect. The problem he's communicating is about those who hid their true motives.

Let's go back to Jude's analogy of the fruitless trees. There was no substance to them despite an appearance contrary. Contrast that with Jesus, who had life-changing substances but didn't always look good. Jude is the brother of James and Jesus, and all had a bend toward action. The result of Jesus' life benefitted every person everywhere for all the time. Jesus says:

"Beware of false prophets who come disguised as harmless sheep but are really vicious wolves.

You can identify them by their fruit, that is, by the way they act. Can you pick grapes from thorn bushes, or figs from thistles? A good tree produces good fruit, and a bad tree produces bad fruit. A good tree can't produce bad fruit, and a bad tree can't produce good fruit. So, every tree that does not produce good fruit is chopped down and thrown into the fire. Yes, just as you can identify a tree by its fruit, so you can identify people by their actions."

Matthew 7:15-20

Jesus leaned into metaphors like his brother Jude does to warn unsuspecting people of the dangers of others who would come in to manipulate and exploit them. He talks about them as wolves who appear as sheep among sheep with the intention of harm. Wolves eat sheep.

None of us are perfect or should pursue perfection, but while we're imperfect, there ought to be some positive and good fruit in our lives due to our faith. What sort of fruit do we produce, as the analogy goes, if we are truly following Jesus? Are we humble? Have we become more faithful? Do we practice generosity? These prove pure motives.

A mistake many of us make is to think that we need to produce better fruit on our own: be a more patient person or have better self-control. We get frustrated when that doesn't happen. Jesus doesn't ever tell us to produce these things on our own, by ourselves. Being a follower of Jesus will cause us to be more faithful,

generous, and humble as we develop a closer relationship with him. Our pursuit as spiritual people is not
one of perfection. It's a relationship with a God who
gave everything up to be with us. The fruit of that pursuit will be evident to everyone around us.

ACTIVATE AUTHENTICITY

We must humble ourselves to recognize how weak we
are and how we may unwittingly become like those
groups Jude talks about. As with everything Jude
writes, or any biblical author, we must consider their
context before ours. We also don't assume they're only
talking about someone else, somewhere else. Whether
or not Jude is writing about a metaphorical wandering
star, Cain, or Israel, we would be wise to recognize the
shortcomings they displayed that life inside of each of
us. In the case of these analogies, we can relate that
much of what goes on in our everyday lives is unseen.

When we show what's going on, we strategically show
the world a little bit of our reality in pursuing an image
of ourselves that others will love and respect. We con-
form to the world's pressures in a certain way, which
leads us to an unhealthy place. When we get there, we
have no choice but to care for ourselves at the expense
of those around us.

The solution to these problems is authenticity. We follow
Jesus with all our flaws to the best of our ability with
transparency and honesty. We humbly admit when
we're wrong and take responsibility for ourselves when
we'd rather blame someone else. Authenticity requires

humility, which comes at the cost of being vulnerable.

That means we must give up our pursuit of perfection and be okay with others doing the same, including pastors and other church leaders. No one is perfect. It's time we stop expecting them, and ourselves, to be. A warning, though: Steward your authenticity well.

Not everyone you encounter needs to know your deepest, darkest secrets. At the same time, someone should. That's the balance and challenge of managing this spiritual discipline. Trusting the right people with your vulnerabilities is freeing. Opening up to the wrong people could exploit you. We must use discernment and pray for God's wisdom as we do so.

HOMEOWNERS IN MADISON

Megan and I have wanted to buy a house in Madison for over five years. We would pray about it and ask others to pray, but something always came up. Sometimes it was our credit scores. Other times, we didn't have enough money saved for a down payment. A lot of times, it was both!

Then, in the middle of the pandemic, we saved enough money and had good enough credit scores to finance a home. The only drawback at that time was that the housing market was about as competitive as ever. Houses in our area were listed on Wednesdays and Thursdays, with offers being accepted the next Monday morning. We would frantically look at pictures to decide whether we wanted to take a closer look with a walk-through on Saturday and Sunday.

There was absolutely no time to prayerfully consider what to offer. We offered $15,000 over the asking price on one house we looked at and loved, only to find out they received 17 more competitive offers and were going with a higher bidder. It was a frustrating time because we were finally able to purchase a house in Madison, but it was during a very competitive season. We began to feel like, once again, we wouldn't be able to close on a home. Something always seemed to come up.

Then, there was a house that caught our eye. It was the largest one we looked at, nearly 2,000 square feet on half an acre lot. It also had the lowest price tag of any of the houses we looked at. We got to walk through, but it wasn't love at first sight for Megan.

The house was cluttered and dirty. It resembled what you'd expect to see on an episode of *Hoarders*. While less extreme than what the reality tv show comes out with, we carefully moved around piles of stuff as we took as close of a look at the house as we could. We put in an offer from the street in front of the house with our realtor right after the showing, and a few hours later, I got an email saying the offer was accepted.

I knew there would be plenty of work to do. The inspection would show as much. Then came the things we needed to learn about after we moved in. During our first weekend there, the house's main drain back flooded. It took two different plumbing companies over three days to fix it.

Sometimes things, like houses, aren't the way they initially seem. People can be the same way. Even if we have an idea about what's wrong, as we had with our house because of the inspection, sometimes things will come up that we didn't know about. When this happens at a societal level, injustice is evident.

CHAPTER 7:
ENOCH'S PROPHECY

2020 wasn't a year only plagued by a new infectious disease. That summer brought greater attention to many of the systemic injustices that have plagued Black people for centuries in the United States. This simultaneously hit a peak in one sense and a low in another when the world, staying at home because of one virus, watched and rewatched another take the life of George Floyd in Minneapolis on May 25.

We heard Floyd beg for his life, exclaiming and then whimpering, "I can't breathe," for nine minutes and 29 seconds before seeing him take his last breath on the street under the knees and weight of four police officers. This type of incident has played out several times in Minneapolis alone in recent years.

Philando Castile was shot and killed during a traffic stop in 2016, right in front of his four-year-old daughter and girlfriend, who captured the tragedy on Facebook Live.

Daunte Wright was killed during a traffic stop in 2021 when a police officer claimed she meant to use her Taser, not her gun.

Amir Locke was killed while SWAT executed a no-knock warrant in 2022 and shot him. Locke was not named on the warrant.

Just like how the Covid-19 virus started in one place and moved in closer as it spread, our ever-increasing awareness of systemic injustices hit closer to home in Madison that summer. On August 23, in Kenosha, Wisconsin, I watched the cellphone footage of Jacob Blake, a Black man, being shot by a police officer in the back seven times while his kids were in the backseat of his car. The attack left him permanently paralyzed. That white police officer was never charged with a crime.

Then, two days later, on August 25, a teenager from Illinois came to Kenosha armed with a semi-automatic rifle someone else bought him since he was too young to buy or possess the weapon. The teen shot three, killing two. While he was charged with several crimes, he was found not guilty of any wrongdoing.

At this point, the law in the U.S. was loud and clear: A white person with a gun could shoot a Black person walking away from them, or a few people protesting said shooting with impunity.

I've grown more confident since 2020 that if there ever was an ideal time in recent history for the white church to find its lost prophetic voice in society, it would've been over that period. It could have been a solid moment to return to relevancy and respectability.

We had the moment to speak life and justice into a nation that lacks both and is sensing something wrong, but we failed. Instead of following Jesus, we followed our favorite TV and radio personalities. We became a collective movement of antagonism against any call to repentance of historical wrongdoing.

"I can't breathe" became a cry for all those, and many of them experienced a form of injustice because of the color of their skin. White followers of Jesus could have attempted to help pull the metaphorical hands of sys-temic oppression off their necks. Still, we chose to have our own hands help tighten the grip.

JUSTICE FOR ALL

Let me be abundantly clear, justice isn't an issue *some* believers should care about, just as racism isn't an issue that affects *some* people. These are not topics *some* followers of Jesus should be knowledgeable about. Injustice and racism are problems that *all* of us who have faith in God should care deeply about because God is the God of justice.

And how we respond to injustice directly reflects the depth and width of our understanding of God's character.

Justice is stated as a central part of Jesus' mission to earth from the very onset of his ministry thousands of years ago. Luke records the moment Jesus publicly says his purpose for the first time. Reading from Isaiah 61 in his boyhood synagogue, Jesus proclaims:

"'The Spirit of the Lord is upon me, for he has anointed me to bring Good News to the poor. He has sent me to proclaim that captives will be released, that the blind will see, that the oppressed will be set free, and that the time of the Lord's favor has come.'"

Luke 4:18-19

Jesus both startles and offends the religious elite of his day by inferring that Isaiah was prophesying about him hundreds of years earlier. They actually try to kill him for the first time after this. Why was this so offensive to them?

Jesus was an absolute nobody at this point.

None of the writers of the biographies of Jesus, the Gospels, say much about his childhood or adolescent years. Apparently, only a little happened that was worth writing about in Jesus' life before he was well into adulthood!

That all changes when he walks into the crowded synagogue and confidently declares that he's the Messiah Isaiah prophesied about hundreds of years prior. They would have been beside themselves when he went further, insisting the Messiah would be "Good News" to those who weren't wealthy, free, healthy, and powerful.

I suspect many believers in the United States would have joined in on this attempt at Jesus' life had we lived at that point in history after hearing this, too. Many would wonder who this nobody thinks they were saying God has come to save the social, political, and economic outcasts over the rest of us.

Does that mean that some people are excluded from the Good News? Absolutely not. But justice is so imperative to the Gospel. Jesus emphasizes that this Good News is first and foremost for those who experience injustice. And if the message of our faith excludes justice, then it's not faith in Jesus.

As we look at the world around us, with all the injustices being broadcasted from every screen we possess, we might think that Jesus failed. He did not. Justice can never indeed be fully served here on this earth. This is Jude's next point.

ENOCH'S PROPHECY

We must remember all these things about Jesus and justice when reading Jude's following few sentences. A clash between God's will and ours (sin) ultimately results in injustice. It's apparent in our society that's going on, but it was also relevant to Jude's original audience. Jude, going back to *1 Enoch* for the third time in this little letter, writes:

"Enoch, who lived in the seventh generation after Adam, prophesied about these people. He said, 'Listen! The Lord is coming with countless thousands of his holy ones to execute judgment on the world's people. He will convict every person of all the ungodly things they have done and for all the insults that ungodly sinners have spoken against him."

Jude 14-15

A bit more about Enoch here than we've gotten into so far. This Enoch is believed by many to be the Ethiopian great-grandfather of Noah. His passing into the next life is recorded in the first book of the Bible: "Enoch walked steadily with God. And then one day he was simply gone: God took him" (Genesis 5:24, MSG).

As far as we're told, and as hard as it is to understand, Enoch never died. His writings, specifically *1 Enoch*, played a significant role in the life of the early Church and its thought processes. Not only does Jude cite it throughout his message, but it was highly regarded by other apostolic leaders at the time.

Before you look for it, *1 Enoch* is not in the Bible as we have it today. It was not in the Bible as they had it 2,000 years ago, either. Using this non-biblical text here was another clever element for Jude to bring up because his audience likely would have had more reverence for Enoch than Paul. They would've been familiar with this story as they were with the earlier story of the dispute over Moses' body (v. 10).

Even though 1 Enoch in its entirety isn't considered inspired text, it served an inspired purpose in Jude. That purpose, at this point, is to show that God is the ultimate provider and enforcer of justice. *Injustice* cannot exist in heaven, where God rules and reigns supreme.

In contrast, hell is where *justice* ceases to exist.

Interestingly, Jesus never talked publicly to the masses about hell. He taught his disciples about it and talked about hell more than anyone else in the Old and New Testaments (about half a dozen times).

MISUNDERSTANDING HELL

As I wrote in the opening of this book, talking about hell is one of the reasons some of us read Jude and decide not to study any further. Like sin, many today misunderstand hell. We commonly imagine a few of us partying in heaven with "streets of gold" and living in "mansions." In contrast, we've been taught that God puts a lot of others in hell to be tortured by fire forever. *This is not a biblical view about the nature of hell.*

A more biblical view of hell is a state of being after death, in which one is permanently separated from God. God doesn't want anyone to be there, separated from him. God's words and actions could not make that message more explicit. It was a message that those who knew Jesus best would write about in their biblical texts.

John writes how Jesus died for the sins of the whole world, and not just a select few (1 John 2:2). Peter wrote that God doesn't want anyone to be "destroyed" and wants all to "repent" (2 Peter 3:9). Paul teaches how God "wants everyone to be saved" (1 Timothy 2:4). God is looking for reasons to get people into heaven, not keep them out—to the point of dying on a cross for those who would reject his love anyway.

And yet, we know that what God wants is not what God gets. The sin that leads to injustice and eternal separation may be why we don't want to read or study Jude, but it's why Jude writes. Heaven is the point of our cosmic timeline where sin and injustice no longer exist. Working for heaven on earth means working toward a world without injustice.

Just as we are to work for heaven on earth, we must recognize that hell is also on earth and that there are many people experiencing it. God didn't accept this, and neither should we. How else should we feel about that except with deep indignation?

God chose Earth with us instead of heaven without us, which is amazing. In doing so, he brought heaven to earth in many ways. Whereas heaven is a promised eternity without pain or suffering, hell is justice served. Writer, poet, and artist Jackie Hill Perry observes these verses in Jude,

> "Imagine if we had a justice system that never executed justice... Where those who have abused the vulnerable, oppressed, the poor and failed to care for the marginalized were never ever confronted about their wrongdoing. At a fundamental level, we'd conclude that a justice system like that was unjust, and if unjust, then not good. This might describe our current justice system and the world in which we live, but it does not and will never describe God."[9]

Those who have brought hell on earth without remorse will be subjected to that reality after death. For people to be able to choose heaven, we must be able to choose hell. Again, Jude doesn't write if this wasn't so. If everyone ended up in the Kingdom of God regardless of our choices, then the spiritual imposters and religious frauds, and not Jude, were correct in their beliefs.

ACTIVATE JUSTICE

I recently received a text message from a volunteer at our church that was so large that it needed to be downloaded as a file to read. (I had a pretty recent iPhone too!) This person, a white guy in his 20's, claimed that I didn't teach about the attributes of God enough. He cited justice as an example in his tirade leading up to the announcement that he would find a new church community. In the following sentence, he accused me of discussing racism too much.

I'm curious if he'll ever see the irony in his writing that day.

We don't just talk about something because a tragedy occurs or because it's featured on the nightly news this week. This sort of "virtue signaling" won't lead to God's desired change. The injustice we're confronting has been going on for hundreds of years. Many others have been fighting for justice for longer than we've been alive. We won't eliminate injustice over a weekend church gathering.

Justice is critical to our faith because it is one of God's

attributes. Still, real justice isn't kicking in the windows of a business, even if it leads to policy changes. It's not in criminal charges, even when a guilty verdict is given. As we've talked about it so far, real justice can only be carried out by God. This, however, doesn't mean we quietly sit on our hands until God's justice is served.

SILENCE IS VIOLENCE

During the summer of 2020, some people from our church, along with my son, Oliver, who was four, marched alongside 10,000 other people of faith in Madison. This large demonstration showed unity between different theological branches of the Christian Church. Oliver proudly held up his "silence is violence" sign as we walked down the historic State Street.

Despite the many issues we could disagree on, we all agreed that justice being served on earth was God's will.

The march ended at the State Capitol building. A prayer service followed on the front steps as many of us mourned and lamented the continued senseless loss of life. That day was one of the most spiritual moments I've experienced, and it continues to impact me today.

We speak up for justice, even when it doesn't directly impact us, because we work toward the Kingdom of God, pursuing God's will here on earth as it is in heaven.

This is in stark contrast to how we've been. Instead of being accountable for our shortcomings, we defer responsibility by pointing the finger at a larger society that doesn't know Jesus as well as we do. The physical and spiritual health and well-being of our families, friends, neighbors, and coworkers depend on it. We must either collectively repent of this or of us who will begin to separate ourselves from those who won't.

BLACK LIVES MATTER

One evening shortly after George Floyd's murder, I got a message from the president and CEO of a large nonprofit inviting me to join him and other community leaders in going downtown Madison. It was rumored that, on this particular night, there would be a lot of unrest.

I recall walking up to the crowd. For blocks, we could see a large group in the street. Many voices of young people in their late teens and early twenties were being broadcasted over a loudspeaker. You could hear the anger in their voices. My heart raced as our small group walked up to them and the unknown of the evening. The narrative the media had convinced me of was that groups like this were up to no good.

The reality couldn't have been further from the truth.

Those who showed up formed a community of young people who were lamenting the reality that their lives meant less than others in the eyes of many. When many declared, "Black Lives Matter," the Christian masses countered, "All Lives Matter." As I listened to what they were saying, I thought about our response, as believers, to what was occurring in the USA.

Which is true for God. *All lives do matter.*

We quickly found out, however, that for many American Christians, life only mattered if they followed specific rules and were white. Let's remember being instructed to indefinitely withhold our judgment when a white person senselessly killed Black people but also told to try to make sense of why a Black woman killed while sleeping in her bed was somehow justified.

Those who vigorously defended some people's rights readily dismissed others, almost always correlating with the color of one's skin. A white person, whether an officer of the law or a kid from out of state, could decide that a Black person wasn't entitled to due process. There was never real substance behind "All Lives Matter." And, as many others have pointed out, all lives can't matter until Black lives do.

FROM *INTENT* TO *IMPACT*

These experiences have led me to a greater, albeit incomplete, understanding of the injustices Black, Indigenous, and People of Color (BIPOC) regularly face. Before 2020, our church would ask a BIPOC pastor to come into our church and speak about racial issues and justice annually. What we were doing seemed more than adequate at the time, especially compared to what other predominantly white churches like ours were doing. We became aware that it was inadequate in creating meaningful change in us and made a series of changes in how our church operated.

We continue to invite BIPOC pastors to teach at our church gatherings, but we do so more often than once a year now. The most significant change is asking them to speak on any topic they desire. Some have chosen to talk about race, but most haven't. That's alright because the point is listening to what they have to say.

Our church moved 10% of our reserves at the church to a Black-owned financial institution. Together with several other churches around the United States, we participated in what we've called #JusticeDeposits, resulting in millions of dollars being moved into Black-owned banks. This initiative helps increase the ability of these financial institutions to give more small business and mortgage loans to populations regularly turned down.

I've been a part of a small group of local pastors who are "leaning into" conversations and initiatives surrounding issues of race and justice. This group was started by a Black-led organization that has been doing this kind of work in Madison for decades. During our time together, we have honest conversations about some of the issues I've written about in this chapter.

Their input has also shaped my writing and theology and my life.

The point in bringing all this up is that it's a process that takes humility and vulnerability. We're all still learning. It isn't just one individual's responsibility to seek justice. It's that of the church community to come together collectively. We don't do this for some diversity tokenism, either.

We want all people to find our faith communities to be places where they can heal and thrive.

TALKING *TO* THEMSELVES, *FOR* THEMSELVES

We are most like Jesus when we work for the justice of others at the cost of our freedoms. It's what he did for all of us. Hell is the physical and spiritual reality if we don't. Jude warns that this will occur more in the faith community if they don't take his warnings seriously.

It's imperative to listen to those around us. If we don't, we create an "echo chamber" in which our beliefs go unchallenged. This is also an issue within Jude's community. Jude continues: "These people are grumblers and complainers, living only to satisfy their desires. They brag loudly about themselves, and they flatter others to get what they want" (**Jude 16**).

Regardless of what we're talking about—justice, authenticity, generosity, humility, or faithfulness—there will be those who grumble and complain about it. They do so whenever the content of the conversation is about selflessness, doing something God's way instead of their own. We can all be like this from time to time, but they do so all the time.

They're inauthentic, greedy, arrogant, unfaithful, and unjust. They *talk* to get what they want, but we *act* to get what God wants. We must have a propensity toward action. Whereas the focus up until this point has been on describing those causing disruption amongst Jude's friends, the direction from here on out will be on helping one another—including those doing harm.

PART 3:

JUDE 17-25

CHAPTER 8:
APOSTOLIC WARNINGS

Less than a year after we launched the church in Madison, we hired a young woman who brought tremendous potential and promise to our team. I met her while coaching at a church planting event she attended. We got together at the end of the day with several others interested in our unique philosophy of ministry.

Only she and her husband felt prompted to move and join us. Hiring her was a big deal because we couldn't pay her anywhere near what she was worth to our team. Our best asset was an unseen vision of what our church community *could* be. As our executive pastor, her primary responsibilities were to help me develop and execute strategies to help our vision become a reality.

That first year of ministry had many ups and downs (more downs than ups) but bringing her into our team was one of the highlights in those early days. I earnestly thought that the two of us would be the right leadership duo for our church to accomplish its mission in Madison. That excitement and hope wore off quickly.

Our working relationship was plagued with immaturity and inexperience. I gave offense quickly. She took offense easily. While we tried to overcome many of our issues, we ultimately couldn't. As time went on, we became toxic together. The only thing we did well was keep our problems between us so that they didn't negatively affect the people we pastored. Eventually, not even that was true.

Almost two years after she moved to Madison, she told me that she had decided to resign. She and her husband would relocate to Atlanta to be closer to his family. This was a perfect way out for all of us. They could be where they wanted to be, and I wouldn't have to make any decisions regarding her job with us.

When neither of them could find work in Atlanta, she wanted to stay in her role at our church longer, which was not an option. We had already transitioned her out, and things were growing healthier in her absence. I had moved on with no desire to return to how things were. This led to hurt feelings, deep wounds, and a ripple effect of division and damage. About one-third of our church's membership left within a few months. Soon after that, they relocated to Atlanta as planned.

It was devastating that this was the reality after having so much hope for what could have been. My faith in what we were doing here came into significant doubt. The division within our church had devastating, real-life consequences. It would take us years to get on the other side of that long summer, and it was the closest I've ever come to quitting since those first few weeks of starting the church.

APOSTOLIC WARNINGS

Jude transitions from Old Testament illustrations for the first time in his message to cite none other than his peers, the apostles. His original audience *should* have known better than to be deceived based on the stories from their history alone, but they didn't. They failed to recognize what was happening around them. As such, Jude writes about more present warnings since the apostles were saying and writing these things during this same era. "But you, my dear friends, must remember what the apostles of our Lord Jesus Christ said..." (**Jude 17**).

In writing these words, Jude subtly elevates the apostles' words to the same level of inspiration and authority as the Hebrew Scriptures (our Old Testament). It's one of those passages that modern readers like us easily miss the significance of. These words were part of the message the original recipients likely struggled with the most because they were primarily Jewish Christians.

For Jude to bring up Moses was to be expected, but citing this ragtag team made up of former fishermen and tax collectors as authorities was not.

The generation Jude belongs to would not live to see the completion of the New Testament. You and I, in stark contrast, live some 1,600 years after its canonization. Almost everyone living in the United States today owns multiple Bibles. Therein lies a big difference in how we might read this verse in Jude versus how the first audience would have.

While it's not his main point, we cannot ignore that Jude, a follower of Jesus, clearly viewed the apostles' words just as important as the Hebrew Scriptures, even though the full extent of that was likely unknown to even him at the time. They would not have easily accepted this, which isn't all that different from objections some have about the biblical texts today.

FAITH THAT PRECEDES THE BIBLE

Some profess that the Bible is why they don't, won't, or can't believe in God. This might describe someone you know and love. Several well-known atheist thinkers cite in their books and teachings that they do not believe in God *because of* the Bible. (When I say this, it always surprises someone who is unfamiliar with atheism, but it's nonetheless true.)

It's entirely unnecessary for several reasons. The biggest of them was that the first followers of Jesus, the kind of communities Jude wrote to, didn't have the Bible and still believed in who Jesus claimed to be. Same with the first disciples. And long before that, God had been pursuing people like Abraham, Joseph, and Moses before one letter was written in the oldest book of the Old Testament.

To put it plainly: The Christian faith precedes the formation of the Bible.

And that faith didn't just exist. It grew *exponentially*—from 120 in the Upper Room after Jesus' ascension to over 3.5 million people by the 4th century. People can find and follow Jesus before accepting the Bible as God's inspired and infallible word. You do not have to believe in the Bible to have faith in God.

Hopefully, at this point in the book, you know that I'm not against the biblical texts or saying we don't need them. The Bible is God's story and a tool that helps us live according to God's will. It's a collection of writings from other cultures, written thousands of years ago by dozens of authors. That makes it difficult to read and easy to misunderstand.

I firmly believe that the Bible in its entirety would've been to Jude's audience's advantage, as it is to ours today, if they had it. Instead of having to wait for the brother of Jesus to write them a note about what's happening around them, they would've had their own Bible and could have read: "They told you that in the last times, there would be scoffers whose purpose in life is to satisfy their ungodly desires" (**Jude 18**).

DAMAGING DIVISIONS

Jude has built a strong case thus far against those who only live for themselves despite *appearing* altruistic. The proof? Division, which resulted within the Christian community Jude writes: "These people are the ones who are creating divisions among you. They follow their natural instincts because they do not have God's Spirit in them" (**Jude 19**).

Divisive behavior can be evidence that people do not possess the actual Spirit of God. Their lives are evidently unredeemed and too natural. If they had God's Spirit in them, they would have some evidence of self-control. Since they have no self-control, it's proof they do not have God's Spirit. They looked down on others, including Jude, for being bound to anything, even God's will. N.T. Wright adds:

> "No doubt the teachers would have said that it was people like Jude himself who caused divisions, by dragging them back to an old-fashioned morality, based on funny old stories in the ancient scriptures rather than on the freedom they had discovered through what they took to be God's grace. But Jesus and his early apostles had given the same warning as those ancient scriptures.... Such people, says Jude, simply do not have God's Spirit, for all they may claim to do so. They are living at the mere human level."[10]

They argued that they were "so full" of the Spirit that they could do whatever they wanted. Jude already called this out at the beginning as a perversion of God's grace. Now he adds that people are not superior, but rather inferior, if they follow natural instincts while ignoring spiritual ones. The way some lived and told others to live proved that they didn't have the Spirit of God, which caused the division.

THE DIVIDED STATES OF AMERICA

In speaking for things Jesus clearly taught about in the past decade, like working for justice and equity, many followers of Jesus in the United States have been accused of selling out, believing lies, or worse. Our country is polarized, but it's not just the Democrats and Republicans. Our churches are divided, with believers attacking other believers because of how they vote. And worse still, some Christians attacked non-Christians for the same reason!

The division didn't begin with the election cycles in 2016 or 2020, but it has been accelerating at breakneck speeds since. This is happening because we let our politics influence our faith more than our faith influences our politics. We've become those Jude warns about as we follow our natural instincts and create divisions.

Imagine a scenario in which two people who lead different churches in the United States came to Jesus with the same question. One is on the staff of a traditional church with conservative political views. The other serves as the pastor at a progressive church with very liberal leanings. They want to know how followers of Jesus should vote in an upcoming election. Both are aware that people will be affected by how their churches vote, and they take that very seriously.

How would Jesus answer them?

Since this didn't happen, we dare not speculate what Jesus *might* say. However, we certainly know what he *wouldn't* say. He wouldn't tell them whom to vote for. Based on every other interaction Jesus had with people, we know his answer to their question would transcend the current political climate.

"THE GREAT COLLABORATION"

Most of us have heard of "The Great Commandment" (Mark 12:29-31): to love God and others with all our heart, soul, mind, and strength. Many of us have heard of "The Great Commission" (Matthew 28:16-20) to go and make disciples of Jesus worldwide. But only a few have heard of "The Great Collaboration." I remember the first time I heard about it. I was at a leadership conference. Two of the keynote speakers taught one of Jesus' final prayer for his followers in John:

> "I'm praying not only for them, but also for those who will believe in me because of them and their witness about me. The goal is for all of them to become one heart and mind—just as you, Father, are in me and I in you, so they might be one heart and mind with us. Then the world might believe that you, in fact, sent me. The same glory you gave me, I gave them, so they'll be as unified and together as we are—I in them and you in me. Then they'll be mature in this oneness and give the godless world evidence that you've sent me and loved them in the same way you've loved me."

> **John 17:20-23 (MSG)**

Jesus could have prayed for anything at this moment when he knew his ministry on earth was coming to an end, and he prayed for his Church's unity. He didn't pray that we would agree on every issue and share in every belief but that we'd be united. Collaboration, a form of unity in action, isn't an option for the Christian

Church—it's a mandate. Jesus doesn't just ask us or tell us to be unified. He prays that you and I will be *so that* we will be evidence to the world that Jesus loves them.

If our unity shows the world that Jesus loves them, then our disunity does potentially irreparable damage.

That's what's at stake when we refuse to work with other believers, even when they think differently about political issues and theological views than us. Our collective mission is so big that we must collaborate with other churches to accomplish it. We need to collaborate with other believers to follow Jesus fully. Can we love each other unconditionally even if we disagree on the best ways to do that?

People far from God want to see believers, regardless of where they go to church, come together for the flourishing of the community. They do not care about the differences in how we think about baptism or the way we do communion. They see people hurting and believe that we can (and should) help them, *even if they don't believe in God.*

Think of how many posts you've seen recently call Christians out for hypocrisy. The world around us knows what we believe and they long for us to live up to our potential. Unfortunately, we often let them down because of our bickering over mostly insignificant beliefs and ways "to do" church. We can do better, and it starts with each of us becoming more prominent collaborative advocates.

Instead of not working with others because of our

differences, we must rally around our shared belief that Jesus wants us to be unified and collaborate for his will to be done on earth as it is in heaven. Unity doesn't mean uniformity. We can be different and still unified. There's profound beauty in diversity and unity, but when we handle conflict the wrong way, it causes division and pain in ways we don't expect. It hurts innocent bystanders.

How do we begin to fix the divide? Jesus teaches us that there is healing power in unity. Jesus doesn't want us to avoid conflict, which isn't healthy. He offers his followers a better way:

> "If a fellow believer hurts you, go and tell him—work it out between the two of you. If he listens, you've made a friend. If he won't listen, take one or two others along so that the presence of witnesses will keep things honest, and try again. If he still won't listen, tell the church. If he won't listen to the church, you'll have to start over from scratch, confront him with the need for repentance, and offer God's forgiving love."

Matthew 18:15-17 (MSG)

Jesus' instructions are simple and have worked for centuries in every culture. Instead of letting our pain bitter up inside of us, we are to choose authenticity and speak up about it. We are to go to the person or people who have hurt us and allow them the opportunity to make it right. As Jesus points out, they may not express remorse or regret, at which point we seek the help of others.

This is the work of unity. Unity takes work. It requires a group of people committed to becoming humble and living for a purpose greater than themselves. How might this have changed interactions amongst believers regarding shutdowns during the pandemic? Unfortunately, it seemed that for many American Christians, the opinions of our favorite news personalities carried more weight than the teachings of Jesus.

We've all contributed to conflict and played a part in causing division. That doesn't mean we don't have God's Spirit within us. How we respond to division does. I wasn't very willing or intentional about following Jesus' teachings about conflict resolution with our executive pastor. No doubt this was wrong and added to the issues our church community would face.

When we make mistakes, we don't wait for someone we've wronged to come and tell us so. Jesus has a different approach for us. He says:

> "This is how I want you to conduct yourself in these matters. If you enter your place of worship and, about to make an offering, you suddenly remember a grudge a friend has against you, abandon your offering, leave immediately, go to this friend and make things right. Then and only then, come back and work things out with God."

Matthew 5:23-24 (MSG)

Essentially, Jesus tells us to think of the most spiritual thing we could do. His example is giving money to a church. To Jesus, being aware of and owning our mistakes and making amends is more important than anything else we could do—no matter how spiritually important it may seem. When we hurt others, we proactively seek healing. This requires us to have already developed a certain level of humility so that we can be accountable.

LEARNING FROM OUR MISTAKES

After that heartbreaking summer in 2017, we made "biblical conflict resolution" a core part of our strategy. You can even see it today on the church's website. What we experienced in Madison was more because we didn't handle conflict in a healthy or wise way. We still have conflict, but we deal more proactively and biblically now. We know conflict will happen, but when dealt with poorly, it divides and inflicts pain on the body of believers and hurts our witness.

I know that I've got to lead the way with this in my personal relationships, but I need accountability because sometimes I don't want to do the work of unity. In my leadership position, I can be lazy—and have been—when it comes to working through conflict. It doesn't always seem worthwhile to me, but Jesus' words tell me otherwise.

A new family from Virginia started coming to our church the same year we hired our first executive pastor. Dan had gotten a job at a local software company. His family hadn't moved to Madison yet, so he was checking out different churches. When his wife and kids relocated here, they got heavily involved in everything we were doing.

He and I wouldn't become close friends until our church was hit with the crisis brought on by division, which was just over two years from when he first visited. During that challenging season, Dan stepped up in ways that most people never would. He helped me personally and assisted in leading our church as we healed from heartbreak. We couldn't have recovered and moved on as well without him.

Dan even took a pastoral role for a season with us and regularly taught during our Sunday gatherings. Whereas we couldn't pay our first pastor *very much*, we couldn't pay Dan *at all*. Despite working a full-time job, having two kids, being married, and having a bunch of hobbies, he set aside upwards of 10 hours a week working with us.

Dan may not have been there on day one, but he's undoubtedly responsible for helping us make it this far since then. Several other people to have their names mentioned as being a critical part of what we do and how we do it—including our executive pastor, who positively impacted many most of her time here while serving in Madison. It would be nearly impossible to give everyone the recognition they rightly deserve.

During the week, they're doctors, educators, stay-at-home-parents, and in business. They have varying degrees of education and backgrounds. Still, they lead our band and small groups, direct our children's ministries, and help set up chairs on Sundays. As a result, upwards of half of our church found Jesus at our church, and we've baptized new believers every year since 2014.

Whereas those without the Spirit of God were creating division, Jude instructs readers, his friends, to build each other up. He says, "But you, dear friends, must build each other up in your most holy faith…" (**Jude 20**). This, however, requires some supernatural intervention.

CHAPTER 9:
REDISCOVERING PENTECOST

During my final semester as an undergraduate student in 2011, I was co-leading a team of my peers to central Jamaica for a service trip over spring break with my friend, Wes. Amid all the planning and preparation for different projects, we were intentional about the time we spent in prayer together.

Around the same time, I was experiencing significant spiritual attacks regularly. I vividly remember sitting at my desk or lying in bed and having that feeling of someone else being in the room with me. The first few times it happened, I thought I was being pranked by friends. Then there were terrible nightmares. Sometimes I didn't even know I was dreaming because they felt so real. I constantly felt that I wasn't safe, like someone or something was trying to hurt me.

It was hard to share what I was going through with anyone. I felt like a child with an active imagination who was afraid of the dark—except I was 22!

I eventually got the nerve to tell Wes about my struggles, which were beginning to affect me physically. He suggested I bring it up during one of our team's prayer meetings. As we prayed for and received prayer from one another during one of those times, it occurred to me that I didn't know specifically what I needed. I believed in spiritual warfare, but what should we have been specifically asking God to do?

That's when some started praying for me to be filled with the power of the Holy Spirit, which I didn't believe would happen. It might've happened thousands of years ago with Jesus' first followers, but it didn't happen in the 21st century.

Or so I thought.

Hours had passed. Things were winding down. I felt more defeated than I had at the beginning of the meeting because *nothing* happened. For a moment, my belief that people weren't filled with the Spirit was more solidified.

Prior to dismissing our group for the night, someone walked up to pray for me one last time. I felt deep in my soul that whatever he was about to say was coming from God. God was going to speak to me through him. He put his hand on my shoulder and quoted Proverbs 3:5 when he said, "Stephen, trust in the Lord with all your heart; do not depend on your own understanding..."

For the first time that night, I told God to do whatever he wanted to even if I didn't believe he would. What happened next was remarkable. It was like my soul left my body and entered the same space as God. I was so overwhelmed by this powerful experience that I had to sit down as it was happening. The thing is, I did not believe this could happen.

Not to me.

Not to anyone else.

When people would talk about being filled with the Spirit, I thought of people who were fanatical or emotional or both. I had put God in a "box" of what I believed was possible, and what happened to me wasn't in that box. My experience forced me to open my mind and expand my theology as to what God could do.

Aside from my first encounter with Jesus, this was the most tangible experience with God I've had in my life. The Holy Spirit filled me to empower me to do what he wanted most from my life. A boldness accompanied me on the way back to my dorm room that evening, and it's still with me today. For the first time in months, I felt comfortable in my home again.

MAKING SENSE OF GOD

We did a series at our church years ago called Making Sense of God. We do studies in which we try to answer people's hard questions about God, Jesus, the Bible, faith, and spirituality every year. I love it when we can answer people's practical questions, like: How can a good God allow pain and suffering? Is the Bible reliable? Do Christians have to choose between faith and science?

But sometimes, when we do series like this, we walk away from them, and we think we've got God all figured out. We *made* sense of God!

While those studies are helpful and good, they can cause us to "box up" God. "Well, now we know everything," we privately conclude. As such, it contributes to a lack of experiences with the supernatural dimension of our relationship with God. We lean on our own understanding at the expense of trusting God.

We will better understand what Jude is about to write next if we can get more background on the Holy Spirit, and specifically how Jude and the first followers of Jesus understood God's Spirit. It is vastly different from what we do today, so we need a little primer on the Holy Spirit.

THE HOLY SPIRIT

We first read about God's Spirit in the first few words of the Bible (Genesis 1:2). As we move forward in time and through the Old Testament, we see the Holy Spirit interacting with God's people in many ways. Moses and David, for example, had the Spirit *on them*. God's Spirit gave unnamed others the inspiration and ability to design the tabernacle. The Holy Spirit had been moving in, though, and around people.

Then, several hundred years before Jude was born, God indicates something is going to change when he speaks through the prophet Joel:

> Then, after doing all those things, I will pour out my Spirit upon all people. Your sons and daughters will prophesy. Your old men will dream dreams, and your young men will see

visions. In those days I will pour out my Spirit even on servants—men and women alike.

Joel 2:28-29 (NLT)

We should find it curious or at least ask *why* God is saying he *will* pour out his Spirit in the future as if it hasn't happened *yet*. This text in Joel makes the claim that there's something *more* to come. For people, primarily Jewish, who lived life according to the Old Testament text, this prophecy would be a sign that the Messiah came and accomplished what God promised he would do for them since the days of Abraham. John the Baptist teaches this sentiment to the crowds coming to be baptized:

> "I baptize you with water; but someone is coming soon who is greater than I am—so much greater that I'm not even worthy to be his slave and untie the straps of his sandals. *He will baptize you with the Holy Spirit and with fire*."

Luke 3:16 (NLT)

Baptism in water is a symbolic act of dying to oneself and being raised to new life, but John says something *and someone* better is coming. Luke writes that John baptized Jesus, and afterward, the Holy Spirit "descended" on him like a dove (3:21-22). Jesus is then described as being "*full* of the Holy Spirit" as he goes into the wilderness to fast and pray (4:1). He returns "*filled with* the Holy Spirit's *power*" (4:14).

Jesus became filled with and was empowered by the

Spirit. This was the launching point for his earthly ministry. He goes on to perform miracles over the next few years, including healing the sick and raising the dead. But then Jesus does what Jesus commonly does, and he tells his followers in John 16:7: "It is best for you that I go away, because if I don't, the Advocate won't come. If I do go away, then I will send him to you."

Can you imagine Jesus himself telling you that it's better for *you* that *he* leaves? Even though the disciples had seen some unbelievable things, hearing this had to be inconceivable. Their lives were forever changed for the better when they found Jesus. How could his leaving be a good thing?

Jesus is referring to the Holy Spirit in this text, indicating that what Joel prophesied and John the Baptist taught still hadn't happened. He doubled down on this message after his death and resurrection. Jesus tells his followers they "will receive power when the Holy Spirit comes upon you..." (Acts 1:8)

And finally, in Acts 2, on the Day of Pentecost, the Holy Spirit filled believers as prophesied and promised. This was the sign, as if there weren't enough already, that Jesus was who he said he was and did what he said he'd do. Those believers were released to go on the mission Jesus told them they would be put on—including Jude, who is noted as being present in the Upper Room when this happened (Acts 1:14).

NATURALLY SUPERNATURAL

The experience changed and shaped him and the others so much that he doesn't feel a need to unpack it as he's done with other topics. Jude's critique of some who rejected the supernatural has been heavy-handed. (He's already called them unreasoning animals!) The alternative is life in the Spirit. Jude writes, "Pray in the power of the Holy Spirit..." (**Jude 20**).

These are the most loaded words in the entire letter for us today. We must seek out being filled with the Holy Spirit so that we can pray in the power of God. God's Spirit is for all of us today. Peter insists this is for everyone: "Each of you must repent of your sins and turn to God and be baptized in the name of Jesus Christ for the forgiveness of your sins. *Then you will receive the gift of the Holy Spirit*" (Acts 2:38).

One benefit is that, in Jesus' words, "When the Spirit of truth comes, he will guide you into all truth..." (John 16:13). What we're missing so much in the world today is the Spirit of Truth. Life is hard, and following Jesus isn't easy. The truth we seek can be elusive at times, but with the power and infilling of the Holy Spirit, we will be able to stand firm no matter what comes our way: "Await the mercy of our Lord Jesus Christ, who will bring you eternal life. In this way, you will keep yourselves safe in God's love" (**Jude 21**).

We've discussed how what we do matters, and how Jude wouldn't have written anything if it didn't. While God keeps us, we have a responsibility in keeping ourselves. Through the promise and power of the Holy

Spirit, we are able to keep ourselves safe in God's love.

CONDUITS OF THE SPIRIT

Throughout the week at the children's home in Jamaica, we helped clean up their property, ran a VBS-type program for the kids who lived there, and worked in their free medical clinic. When on this kind of trip, people leave their home country and are immersed in an entirely different culture. As such, we experience God in different ways.

As a leader of this trip, I wanted to take advantage of that and put an emphasis on the team's spiritual experience. At the end of every night, after we were done working, we would come back, have dinner and play games. Then, we would have a long moment, usually around eight o'clock at night, to pray for each other. We would share what we saw God was doing in and around us throughout the day.

There was one night that sticks out to me to this day. We were praying for Wes's brother in a way to which a lot of us can relate. He just wanted to have a break-through with God. If you've ever felt stuck at some point in your journey of faith or like your relationship with God was stagnant, then you know firsthand what we were praying for. We believed it would happen, and so we started praying for him.

And we kept praying.

And we prayed some more.

And after praying for a while, probably the better part of an hour, we all started to feel a little stuck. We frequently glanced around the room at each other, wondering why it wasn't happening. Wes's brother was frustrated, and the team was discouraged. We'd already seen God do some amazing things through prayer, but this seemed like a low point.

But while we were praying for him, I felt early on that God had put something on my heart or in my mind to share. I didn't want to, though. I wasn't sure it was *really* from God. If it was God, I was certain he chose the wrong person to do it. But with the pressure building, I reluctantly shared what was on my heart.

With my hand on his shoulder, I said, "I think that God is telling me something. He wants you to have a breakthrough, but something in your life keeps you from having it. I don't know what that is. There's something you haven't surrendered to God. He wants you to surrender that, and you'll have your breakthrough as soon as you surrender."

I didn't know what I was talking about, but he did. He fell on his knees, opened his arms, and cried. At that moment, it was like you could see God there. Just like in the Upper Room 2,000 years ago, the Holy Spirit poured out in a little shack in Central Jamaica.

REDISCOVERING PENTECOST

The challenge of this passage in *Jude* is to let God expand what we believe he can and wants to do. We're meant to experience the supernatural activity of God in our lives every day. It's so important that it was better for us that Jesus left. The Holy Spirit fills and empowers us to accomplish the tasks God has set before us.

The Apostle Paul has an interaction with believers in Ephesus about the Holy Spirit, which may be like one he'd have with us today. He asks them if they received the Holy Spirit when they first believed, and they tell him they have not even heard of such a thing (Acts 19:2).

These people were believers who had been baptized in water prior to meeting Paul but had no knowledge and weren't filled with the Holy Spirit. This changes when Paul prays for them. They are filled with the Holy Spirit and begin prophesying and speaking in tongues (Acts 19:6).

Now imagine what you would say or how you would respond to Paul if he asked, "Did *you* receive the Holy Spirit when you believed?" I would have to tell him no, and it wasn't for several years after I first believed that I did. If I were feeling *really* honest, I would tell him I didn't believe I could receive the Holy Spirit until after I did. I'm glad God proved me wrong.

The Holy Spirit is beyond scientific understanding and the laws of nature. For something to be supernatural, it is, by definition, *beyond* the natural. It's outside of what's observable, measurable, and predictable, so many of us struggle to accept it as a reality.

We're okay with the *natural*, even though there are some things about it that we'd like to give up. When it comes to the supernatural part of our faith, a lot of us are hesitant to explore more. There are many reasons, but I have one reason we should open more: By putting God in a box of whatever we deem plausible, we're limiting what he can do in our lives.

God has way better plans for your life than you do, and what's going to make you happy and give you peace. By opening to the Holy Spirit, we are giving God permission to do more in our lives than we can imagine. We're not trying to use God or make something happen because we want to see something happen. That's not it at all. The point is to pursue God's presence and open ourselves up to his will. Experiencing supernatural power is part of that pursuit.

It'll put you at ease to know that even the Early Church, with all of the signs, wonders, and miracles, struggled with the supernatural. It's beyond what people can reasonably comprehend. Jude addresses their doubt and disbelief over it on multiple occasions.

Our journey into the supernatural will undoubtedly feel awkward at times. It's been said that there's no growth without awkwardness. You're not going to become a religious weirdo if you do this. Instead, you'll be amazed at how God's Spirit can move in and around you. Up to this point, whatever age and stage you are, imagine that there's just *one more* thing that God wants to do in your life supernaturally.

We can live supernaturally, in a very natural way.

All you've got to do is unbox God.

This is the way of Jesus. When Jesus came to earth, our supernatural God stepped into the natural world. Jesus wasn't just fully man, but he was also fully God. Jesus supernaturally put the natural world back in order as it was intended. This is what Jude calls us to do next.

CHAPTER 10:
"LOVE THE SINNER, HATE THE SIN"?

We live in an era in which it's not uncommon for popular and well-liked "celebrity pastors" to be removed from their positions because of abuse or neglect. Some of them have used their jobs in the church to leverage sexual relationships, while others spiritually and emotionally manipulate through fear, shame, and guilt. Some even embezzle hundreds of thousands of dollars from the churches they lead.

These are *extreme* examples of what can happen and represent a tiny sect of all clergy. Still, there is something for the rest of us to learn from their often-public shortcomings. Failing morally can happen to anyone, but it hurts everyone.

The Rise and Fall of Mars Hill, a podcast released over several months in 2021, tells the story of a church that started with a dozen or so people and grew into a church with tens of thousands of attendees in dozens of locations across the USA. Mars Hill Church was one of North America's largest and fastest-growing churches when it closed suddenly in 2014. Years of scandals became too much to overlook—even for those who didn't want to look.

The podcast captured a large audience and got us all talking about what happened at that church. We were appalled by their pastor's abusive actions, but the podcast also showed us the people behind his abuse. They are real people who were misled by someone Jude would characterize as a shameless shepherd.

It made the story more heartbreaking to hear the stories of those who were deeply hurt. Many of them are still dealing with the trauma years later.

As I listened to the podcast, I wondered why so many people involved in the church didn't do anything to confront the apparent abuse around them. How could they know what was going on and ignore it?

Their "brand" was unapologetically chauvinistic, citing some passages in the Bible that seemed to defend it. While the messaging drew large crowds, it perpetuated toxic masculinity and a culture of rape.

They called it "the gospel," but it was not the Gospel of Jesus Christ.

The stories from the podcast warned us to look deeper, use discernment better, and define success more biblically. Some people in positions of power *only appear* to be successful and doing everything right. The reality is nowhere near that.

CANCEL CULTURE

Jude transitions to how we ought to respond to those

who have fallen or are drifting in the differing ways we've talked about so far. Jude implores readers and hearers to ensure *their* faith is secure. We cannot give others what we do not possess. We would be wise to put ourselves in a position to heed Jude's instructions to reach out to help those struggling.

But before we go *there*, we must go *here*...

It has been called many names in the past and will be called something else in the future. What is known as "cancel culture" today is a tactic many, regardless of religious views, use to define, shame permanently, and even shun someone based on their worst moments and mistakes. While it has momentum and support, *cancel culture* is antithetical to the Gospel of Jesus that Jude seeks to defend.

Our spiritual adversary would prefer to have all of us defined by our worst mistakes. It's the voice that tries to keep us trapped in our failures when we start to heal and progress, hoping to keep us down and out. Worse, fear of being "canceled" keeps us from addressing real issues. Why would we ever seek help from someone if there's a good chance they will use our shortcomings against us?

When followers of Jesus participate in cancel culture, we are accomplices of the one whom Jesus warns has a mission to steal, kill, and destroy all of us (John 10:10). We don't spiritualize our decision to "cancel" by ripping Jesus' words out of context when he says, "shake the dust from your feet" when someone rejects us (Matthew 10:14).

Now, you might think I'm saying people shouldn't take responsibility and be held accountable. *I've written exhaustively about both those subjects already,* as that's been Jude's primary focus. The pastor of the church in Seattle from the podcast was anything but repentant for the damage he caused and the lives he wounded. As such, we should be cautious of him and anything with which he is associated.

After someone has taken responsibility and has been held accountable, we are to do the work of helping people be better. We are not to break someone down and rid the world of them. Our role is to partner in their rehabilitation. This is in an impactful way that you and I get to play a part in God's redemption and is a distinctly Christian approach. We don't cancel people. We participate in their reconciliation.

The world around us may not understand why we would do things this way. They may even critique us for it. This is the difference Jesus makes in and through us. If that makes you uncomfortable, good; the incredible depth of God's grace should make us all feel uncomfortable.

God sees everything we do and doesn't let our worst mistakes define any of us. God doesn't just see beyond them. He uses them to propel us into a future we could never have imagined. Our failures can be either the wind in our sails or an anchor holding us in place, depending on the perspective of our faith.

Before we think that we would never do, think, or say what someone else did, who now deserves to be "canceled," let's be humble enough to acknowledge that many of us are fortunate enough to live our entire lives without large numbers of people knowing the worst thing we said, thought, or did.

"LOVE THE SINNER, HATE THE SIN"?

At this point in our reading, Jude instructs us to care for those who are off course cautiously. It's not "canceling" them. Jude leans into different categories as he presents a different approach depending on how far one has wandered. There's not a one-size-fits-all approach.

The first group Jude writes about is those who are influenced by false teachings but have not committed to them. These are those who have experience in and around the faith but are beginning to drift off course. For them, Jude writes: "And you must show mercy to those whose faith is wavering" (**Jude 22**).

Jude believes a loving, merciful approach can stop those who have faith from growing apart from God. We must not ignore or reject those struggling. The followers of Jesus to whom Jude writes clearly knew Jude cared about them. Jude doesn't have to follow up everything he says with a statement reminding readers that he loves them. And even though it's not a long message, they're still reading, still listening.

Similarly, we can help those around us who are struggling by loving them well. If we have to tell people we're saying this or doing that "out of love," then we haven't done the work of love yet and should keep whatever it is we think is essential to ourselves. We know this to be true. None of us care what someone else knows until we know they care about us.

Jude wants us to take a more proactive approach with this next group: "Rescue others by snatching them from the flames of judgment" (**Jude 23**). If there is no interruption in their lives to disrupt the trend, they will end up forever apart from God. We cannot give up on them. There's an urgency behind Jude's message. Whether these are the people in our lives who have intentionally walked away from faith or have done so unintentionally because no one showed them mercy, we are to do something about it now.

If we don't, they will experience the pain associated with being separated from God. This occurs after death, as we commonly think it will. In the life after this one, the "fire" purges the world of evil. (I do not take this to be a literal fire, but a metaphorical one as it is usually used in biblical texts.) It also happens now. In this present life, there are real-life, negative consequences to living outside of God's will that hurt. Sin causes actual damage to our lives.

Jude ends his typical triad with those committed to spreading their flawed beliefs. Absolutely referring to those who are now using their influence to point people away from Jesus, Jude writes: "Show mercy to others but do so with great caution, hating the sins that contaminate their lives" (**Jude 23**).

This New Testament passage has undoubtedly inspired the modern catchphrase, "Love the sinner, hate the sin." Most have heard this phrase used almost exclusively when hurtfully calling out something about someone else. However, let's note that is *not* what Jude is saying to do.

(Go ahead and reread it if you don't believe me.)

Jude is not giving us a script to start a challenging conversation with or an idea for a bumper sticker. It's not meant to make us feel better for being mean. His entire message has been a "how to" guide in protecting ourselves from lies and is directed at and written to those discerning what truth is.

The instruction here is for how we are to behave amid conflict and confusion. Jude wants readers to show mercy to everyone, including those who may be a threat to our faith. People are never beyond redemption, but we should protect ourselves from the potential eternity-altering teachings and lifestyles while loving them to the best of our ability. Recall how many people experienced the consequences of those around them because they didn't take precautions.

When others are fighting about how to vote or whether to cooperate with health orders during a pandemic or how we should treat people who disagree with us, those who take Jude's words to heart are to be the voice of reason. Just as it was when Jesus spoke, our contributions to conversations should be transcendent. We're firm in our pursuit of the truth while showing mercy to those we disagree with. We can only do this if we love people as Jesus did.

THE LAW & GOSPEL

Because believers haven't done this well, we're seeing people leave Christian communities hurt. As a result, they're deconstructing their faith as they confront discrepancies between what they learned growing up in and around the church with how people treat one another. The version of Christianity the world sees in us doesn't look enough like Jesus when it should look *exactly* like Jesus.

We need to make sure our traditions are still in line with the teachings of Jesus. Sometimes something that starts off as a good idea, stops being one. When religious leaders were trying to trap Jesus by asking him what he thought was the most important commandment in the Hebrew Scriptures, he responds:

> "'Love the Lord your God with all your passion and prayer and intelligence.' This is the most important, the first on any list. But there is a second to set alongside it: 'Love others as well as you love yourself.' These two commands are pegs; everything in God's Law and the Prophets hangs from them."

Matthew 22:37-40 (MSG)

In Jesus' own words: Every "do" and every "don't" in our Old Testament is about guiding humanity to love God and each other better. Being Jesus' follower is not measured by how many times a day you pray or how much of the Bible you have memorized, but rather about how well we love people—*especially those who are difficult to love.*

If we think we're doing something right, but it doesn't help us love God or other people better, then it's wrong. Again, sin is about more than just the things we shouldn't do. It's about the distance it puts between God and us and each other. Jesus confronts a group of religious elites who were better than most at keeping the rules but who didn't understand why the laws existed in the first place.

WE NEED THE LOCAL CHURCH

It's more evident here than anywhere else in Jude's talk how important the local church is to modern believers. Whatever church we commit to should help us live out our faith between Sundays. None of us are above or beyond having our faith waiver because of our sins or the sins of others. If it hasn't happened to you already, it will. If it has already happened, it will happen again. This is precisely why we need each other.

Many people we've met in Madison through our church are lonely and isolated. It's not that they're unlikeable people. Many of them haven't had to make friends since kindergarten. Now that they've moved to a new city for a job or college, developing strong friendships is hard. I know this to be true because I relocated here and have faced similar challenges.

Interestingly, a lot of people who connect with us in Madison have a traditional or liturgical church background. This is a little strange because our church cannot be described as either of those things. I used to describe our nondenominational church to new people as "disorganized religion."

In learning about them, I've come to find out that most grew up being forced to go to churches they didn't like. They had to overcome hurdles to experience God. If this describes you at this point in your life, I want nothing more for you than to find a life-giving church community.

I must clarify something here. I am not trying to disparage traditional or liturgical churches. I found Jesus at a traditional church, as did many people I know and love. My point is tradition and liturgy are only as good as they help us love people and God better. If they don't, then we've fallen into the same trap as the first-century religious leaders.

THE CHURCH AT ITS BEST

I met my friend Jason almost immediately after I moved to Wisconsin. He invited me to join him and about a dozen other church leaders and pastors from the area for a weekend retreat at a lake house an area businessman let us use. Jason had recently taken the job of Senior Pastor at Wisconsin's largest church, and he was putting together a network of churches that would share resources to accomplish our collective goals.

The annual retreat was intended to help us build relationships and strategize so that we would plant more churches. We hadn't started the church in Madison yet, and I reveled at the opportunity to spend time with other pastors who had done what we were seeking to do.

Over time, Jason became a close friend. He and I met often to talk about family and church life. One time, we met at a coffee shop to discuss the ongoing issues with the executive pastor from earlier. As we talked, I explained to Jason that everything felt more difficult than it should have been because I was so tired.

Our son was about six months old and learning to fall asleep on his own in his crib, but the bedrooms in our apartment got hot at night in the summer. The building had no central air to cool it down. Our only air conditioning unit was attached to a wall at the front of our apartment, away from the bedrooms. We put fans in the windows, but they didn't help much.

After hearing this, Jason abruptly moved the conversation from the coffee shop to his car as we drove to his home in Milwaukee. Once we got to his house, he took out a barely used air conditioner from a hallway closet and gave it to me. It was generous and unexpected. He didn't offer to pray for us or simply write a check. Jason literally gave us an air conditioner he owned but wasn't using. This meant so much to us.

We put the unit in our son's room, which helped us all sleep better at night and enabled me to function better even though the situation with the other pastor continued to spiral.

Years after that, I got a call from a mutual friend who

told me Jason was going to resign from his position, citing multiple infidelities in the letter he wrote to the church. His picture would end up being on the cover of the Milwaukee Journal Sentinel that weekend, along with a copy of his letter. Whereas I've read about mega-church pastors having moral failures plenty of times, Jason was a friend, and it hit differently. I was devastated for him, his family, and the church he once led.

Jason went to rehab immediately after resigning, and I believed that he was taking his recovery from addictions seriously. I invited him to speak at our church nearly two years after his resignation. It would allow Jason to tell his story. I also hoped it would be a chance for him to begin again.

My friend who once spoke to nearly 10,000 people every weekend seemed nervous to talk to the 30 or so who showed up for our evening gathering that Sunday. The weekend he came to speak was before everything shut down because of COVID-19. He shared how his untreated addiction cost him nearly everything.

Shortly after that Sunday, our church community decided to hire Jason part-time. He became a regular teacher and helped our church develop leaders. His faith may have been wavering, but through mercy, we've been able to help him get back up on his feet.

Jason helped me when I felt down and out. When I questioned my worth and calling, Jason stepped up. He met with me, encouraged me, and gave us an air conditioner. There was never any hesitation on my part when he was down and out that I would return the favor.

The Church at its best is about helping one another when we're in need. We show each other mercy because we love others as Jesus does. No matter how big or small or private or public our shortcomings are, we give and receive help from those who won't "cancel" us because we believe in a God who redeems and restores.

CHAPTER 11:
SACRED WORDS FOR MODERN ACTIVISTS

Only a few people do the whole high school thing well. I wasn't one of them. Every day I had to go to school was a bad day. I wasn't a standout artist, athlete, or academic. My clothes were too baggy, my hair was a shaggy mess, and my face was covered in acne. I got bullied a lot too.

The most memorable occasion was when an ex-girl-friend and her friends made and distributed ribbons on a day they dubbed "National Hate Stephen Day." Even though only a few were involved, it might as well have been the whole high school. Stuff like this led to me skipping a lot of school days.

(Go figure, right?)

The punishment was detention. I spent 30 minutes in a small room in the main office almost every Monday, Wednesday, and Friday before or after school. When I hit a certain threshold of detention time that I couldn't make up before the school year ended, I was required to attend a four-hour "Saturday school" detention. I skipped one of those one time and got an in-school suspension for a day as a result.

I can recall hearing adults telling my peers and me that our time in high school was going to be the best time of our lives, and that made me not want to live long enough to find out. It's the only time in my life that I've felt that way.

During one of my final semesters, I took a seat in the middle of a history class. I specifically sat there because I wanted to get through every day as unnoticed as possible. We were a small school, so this was easier said than done. Funny enough, I didn't recognize the girl sitting in front of me in this class. It would turn out she had a similar desire to go as unnoticed as possible and was evidently better at it than me.

We began talking in class often, mostly connecting over our shared disdain for the town we lived in (as teenagers in small towns do). I eventually asked her out, but her parents would let us date only if I went to church. I liked her so much that going to church once a week for an hour or so to be with her seemed like a fair compromise. The midweek youth group would count toward that too.

She and I started seeing each other almost daily outside of school, and I was going to church twice a week by the end of summer. That fall, the youth pastor, Don, took a bunch of teenagers to a weekend fall retreat in Des Moines, Iowa. He and my girlfriend invited me to go, but that seemed way too "Christian" for me at the time. I told both I wouldn't go. She accepted my decision, but Don was more insistent.

He told me I'd have a lot of fun because all we would do was play in sports tournaments and watch music competitions. I thought about it and decided a free weekend playing basketball at a nice hotel with my girlfriend wasn't the worst way to spend my time.

But Don lied to me.

We didn't just play sports and listen to music.

At the end of each day, there was a church service of sorts. A band played music while people worshiped and prayed. Then a speaker came up to talk. He was hilarious, and his messages were deeply challenging.

As I listened over the weekend, I felt convicted about my awful attitude toward others and bad behavior. I became painfully aware that what started off to protect myself from people who hurt me ended up being a way I hurt myself and those closest to me.

During the last song after the message on the last day of the retreat, a friend asked me if I would go to the front with her to pray with someone because she didn't want to go up alone. I agreed, but as I walked up with her, I felt the Holy Spirit calling me. Of course, I didn't know that at the time. I just felt this overwhelming presence that broke through my being as I sensed God fill me with feelings of both worth and value.

I knelt at that makeshift altar and sobbed until the band stopped playing and the lights were turned on. The custodial staff began cleaning up for the night. I was the last student there. What God did in and through me that evening was help me die in the past before he raised me to a new life in the present and future. It has been one of the best and most important moments of my life

When I got up and started to walk back toward my room, the first steps of the rest of and best parts of my life. I glanced back and could see the silhouette of the person I left behind kneeling at that altar. It's a memory I can never forget.

SACRED WORDS FOR MODERN ACTIVISTS

Jude doesn't end his letter like many of his peers in the New Testament do, sending a longlist of greetings or writing out a wordy prayer. Just as promptly and simply as he began, so he ends. Reminiscent of the vernacular from verse one, Jude starts his well-known doxology this way: "Now all glory to God, who can keep you from falling away..." (**Jude 24**).

In a short amount of time and space, Jude brought up story after story and the example of God instructing people to do one thing and them doing another—from people like Cain, Balaam, and Korah, to groups like the Israelites, fallen angels, and Sodomites. He references *1 Enoch*, stories about the dispute over Moses' body, and the Hebrew Scriptures. Jude warns against sin and hell.

After everything he has said so far, with their real and potentially eternal consequences, Jude reminds ancient hearers and modern readers of the certainty of God's powers when he says God can keep everyone and anyone from falling away. We have a God who's more powerful than anything in all creation during our internal and external challenges. While God doesn't always get what he wants, in the end, he is still God. Professor and author Douglas J. Moo writes,

> "Think of the marvelous security promised to us in verse 24: God is able to preserve us so that we can stand before him on the last day spotless, forgiven, assured of an eternal' home in the heavens.' Doubt and anxiety are constant companions on our earthly pilgrimage. We worry about our health, about money, about our children, about our jobs. In sober moments we perhaps become anxious about death. God does not promise to take away these worries, but he does take away from us our greatest worry: where we will spend eternity. Do we reflect this confidence in the way we live? Do we truly value heaven enough so that our earthly worries, while sometimes pressing, fade in importance in light of our eternal destiny?"[11]

When we enter the other side of eternity, we enter existence without pain or suffering. Death will be nothing but a memory of a life lived long ago. God doesn't just keep us from falling away. That would be more than we deserve in many cases, but God has something better for us than just getting by. Jude says God: "will bring you with great joy into his glorious presence without a single fault" (**Jude 24**).

As he concludes this message, Jude assures us that God will bring us into his presence without a single fault and that he'll do so with great joy. When we follow Jesus, as imperfectly as that might be, God will keep us from falling away when it matters most—and doing so makes him happy.

God wants to do this for us. *He literally died for it.* God didn't exempt himself from the pain and suffering of this life. Jesus did life on earth as a subjective participant, not as an objective observer from the spiritual realm. He did this so that one day we would live in a world where people will only choose love.

WORSHIP, ACCORDING TO JESUS

How are we to respond at this point, as we conclude *Jude*? It's through worship. In our modern society, worship often gets diluted into a genre of music or something we do at church. Worship includes those things, but it's so much more. It's also the clothes we put on, the food we eat, and how we respond to other drivers on our morning commute.

Everything we say, think, and do is worship. The only question is who do we worship? Some of the original recipients worshiped themselves. Many American Christians today worship policies or platforms or politicians. They invest their time and money into them. Their moods change based on how well (or not) they do. Our allegiance is to Jesus alone. It's time that we refocus on who we worship.

Jude again emphasizes that Jesus is Lord, adding that he alone deserves our worship: "All glory to him who alone is God, our Savior through Jesus Christ our Lord" (**Jude 25**). I love the way Eugene Petersen paraphrases Paul's words about worship in his letter to the Christians in Rome:

> "So, here's what I want you to do, God helping you: Take your everyday, ordinary life—your sleeping, eating, going-to-work, and walking-around life—and place it before God as an offering. Embracing what God does for you is the best thing you can do for him. Don't become so well-adjusted to your culture that you fit into it without even thinking. Instead, fix your attention on God. You'll be changed from the inside out. Readily recognize what he wants from you, and quickly respond to it. Unlike the culture around you, always dragging you down to its level of immaturity, God brings the best out of you, develops well-formed maturity in you."

Romans 12:1-2 (MSG)

Because God gave up everything for us, our response is to give up everything for God. We take every seemingly insignificant breath and offer it fully and completely to God. We see nothing as unimportant because it's all something we're offering to God, who has everything. Jesus teaches us something else about the nature of worship:

> "It's who you are and the way you live that count before God. Your worship must engage your spirit in the pursuit of truth. That's the kind of people the Father is out looking for:

those who are simply and honestly themselves before him in their worship. God is sheer being itself—Spirit. Those who worship him must do it out of their very being, their spirits, their true selves, in adoration."

John 4:23-24 (MSG)

Here, Jesus states that we must pursue God in *truth* as *worship*. Truth is a central theme of Jude's letter and this book, and it's an aspect of how we are to worship God. When we seek truth, as we have been throughout this reading, we find Jesus, and that's an act of worship.

When we take Peterson's paraphrased words of Paul and Jesus and put them together, we get the most complete understanding of biblical worship I can come up with: "Your everyday, ordinary life—your sleeping, eating, going-to-work, and walking-around life... must engage your spirit in the pursuit of truth."

Putting into practice what we learn from reading and studying *Jude* isn't just good for ourselves; it's honoring God. It's the kind of worship he seeks from his people. It's a lifelong pursuit that changes lives and transforms the world. If we don't worship God, we will worship something or someone else. To worship is a part of who we are and how we were created to be.

Jude ends his inspired message with his own blatant declaration of worship in a statement many churches use to close their services today: "All glory, majesty, power, and authority are his before all time, and in the present, and beyond all time! Amen." (**Jude 25**). This is quite the turnaround from someone who grew up with Jesus and didn't believe he was whom he claimed to be until after his life, death, and resurrection!

A TRIP TO JUAREZ

After returning from that weekend retreat, where I decided to follow Jesus, I remained passionate. That small church in rural Iowa I began going to out of obligation became my spiritual home, and they rallied around me. The following summer, Don took the youth group on a trip to serve in Juarez, Mexico. It still comes to my mind as one of my life's most rewarding yet challenging times.

It was the first time I had been out of the country, and it was my first time traveling without my parents. After arriving in El Paso, Texas, the airline lost my luggage with all my bedding. Once we crossed the border into Juarez, there was hardly any running water or working electricity. We were bunked inside the side of a hill. We were only allowed to take one shower that week, although we certainly needed to do so more often than that!

We were locked in from the outside each night for our safety. (In 2005, Juarez was one of the most dangerous cities in the world.) It was hot every day, there was basically no airflow anywhere, and we could hear, if not feel, the cockroaches looking for something to eat as we lay in bed. This only kept us from staying asleep the first night, as we were too exhausted to care for the rest of the trip!

We spent our days building a roof over a house that didn't have one, helping at a local church's summer camp, and leading a midweek church service for the neighborhood. It was physically and emotionally demanding but pushed me toward a deeper connection with God. When the week was over, and we were back home in Iowa, I knew I had to live this way for the rest of my life.

A few weeks after the trip, Don asked me to lead the church's youth band. I was an inexperienced guitar player with no leadership experience, but I stepped into the role. Don saw something in me I couldn't yet see in myself. It wasn't an easy task, and there was some conflict, but with the help of a youth leader named Tim, I became a good guitar player and a much better leader.

At the end of the year, I went on the annual senior retreat. During this weekend away, Don would intentionally spend one-on-one time with each student to say goodbye. In our time together, I remember him communicating that God must have big plans for my life because of how fiercely he pursued me despite my own resistance.

And even though that relationship with the woman who sat in front of me in history class didn't last, my life hasn't been the same since. My transformation into the person I am today was not immediate.

Early on, when we first come to faith, breakthroughs occur more often than they do later. In my first year of following Jesus, between the retreat, the service

trip, and leading the band, I experienced many positive changes. The changes have taken a lot more time
as time has passed. The most frustrating thing about
faith is that our ideas change faster than our habits do.

I would spend the better part of the next decade
coming up short with my pride, anger, and bitterness.
When I feel like I've surrendered all I must give back
to God, I find a different part of my life I wasn't even
aware of. That's precisely why we do what we do in
committing to God, following Jesus, and being led by
the Holy Spirit.

CONCLUSION

I chose to begin a seven-part teaching series through Jude in *July* of 2018. I didn't think most people in our church community would be interested in going word-by-word through this odd page in the New Testament when we could study more well-known works written by the likes of Peter, James, and John. But I was wrong about the response we would receive.

Whereas people usually have packed weekend plans during very short Wisconsin summers, attending our church gatherings for the *Jude* series on Sunday mornings was worked into calendars, alongside going to local festivals and trips to the lake. The study ended up being one of the most popular we've ever done in Madison, as evidenced by podcast downloads, video views, and consistent turnouts during our weekend gatherings.

It was unexpected!

After our teaching series through *Jude* was finished in August 2018, a few close friends suggested I write this book. It wasn't much, but it was all the encouragement I needed to do something (I already wanted to do). You're holding the finished product now, but it took a great deal of time to get here.

I began writing, but quickly got stuck and quit. I didn't return to this project for another two and a half years.

In January 2021, I felt it was the right time and that I had to do this. Now it's something I've done!

I've been praying for you, the reader, and every word I, the writer, have put in this book. My intention has never been to write a bestseller or make some money. (I think there would've been easier ways to do the latter!) I'm only motivated by the possibility that I may positively impact your journey in following Jesus. That's why I do what I do every day.

As you finish reading and I write this, we are preparing to set it down for the last time. Let's take a moment to reflect and respond to what God may have been speaking to us throughout it. The ideas that Jude taught about, that I've written about, and that you're reading about will take time to put into practice. Faith is a journey, not because we must earn acceptance, but because the God we follow is always on the move. This makes hearing from and responding to God just as important today and tomorrow as it was yesterday.

WHAT'S GOD SAYING TO YOU?

Every week at our church in Madison, we end our gathering time with this question: "What's God saying to you?" In a society that encourages, and even celebrates, being busy and rushing from one thing to the next, it's critical to our holistic health to slow down. It's essential to have regular moments to reflect on what God might be saying or how God might be attempting to lead us. This is counter-cultural in the best way possible.

Perhaps God spoke to you regarding how you're called and kept in his love. You can rest assured that your identity isn't found in what you do but to whom you belong. It doesn't matter how often you've failed in the past because God is still doing his best work in and around you. That we must experience death for us to have a new life.

Or maybe you felt God speaking to you about a specific action. Which of the five disciplines discussed in this grouping of chapters (faithfulness, authenticity, generosity, humility, and justice) could you improve upon the most? Practically speaking, what could you do today or this week to get started?

Could it be something about helping someone else in your life find and follow Jesus? When our faith feels stagnant, helping someone else with theirs helps us. It's time to help others struggling with their faith all around you. Is there a name of a person who kept coming up that you should reach out to for a conversation about spirituality?

Professor Rebecca Skaggs offers a series of additional questions we can consider after studying Jude:

> "To what extent is God truly Lord of my life? Do I really submit to his authority in my daily decisions and interactions with others? To what extent does my life reflect the love and mercy of God in my dealings with others? How do I relate to those who do not acknowledge the lordship of God? Do I ignore their stance in order to make life more peaceful? Do I find

myself compromising in order not to confront them? Do I even find myself slipping into patterns of behavior that do not reflect the lordship of God?"[12]

So, again, what's God saying to you? I've come to find in being a pastor for over a decade that God is almost always speaking to us. Throughout this reading, God was probably talking to you about many other aspects of your life. Still, it's hard to hear from God if we don't recognize his voice. Thankfully, it's a skill we can develop.

HOW TO HEAR FROM GOD

Every time Megan was pregnant with one of our kids, I would talk to them. They didn't even have ears at that point! Then, after they were born, I continued to speak to them even though they didn't understand what I was saying. They would just cry if they were hungry, sleepy, or needed a diaper change. Sometimes, they cried for no reason at all.

As they got older, they were able not only to listen but talk. (I've been told at some point that they'll even begin to develop the ability to talk back to me!) It started with "dada," and then their words for "bottle" and "pacifier." Eventually came "Mama." Then they began stringing words together to form sentences. Only their mom and I would know what they were saying early on. We only knew because we were listening for certain words and guessing what they wanted to say.

We go to Walt Disney World about every other year,

courtesy of my parents. Despite there being 100,000 other people there with all sorts of music playing and rides going, all I have to do is say their name, and they can recognize my voice. If our oldest, Oliver, was walking too far ahead or behind, I would say, "Oliver," and he would look for where the voice was coming from to find out what I wanted to tell him.

(This is different from Elijah, who hears my voice and decides not to listen anyway!)

The calm voice of their dad cut through all the other loud noises around them. My intent in calling them was to stop them from getting lost in the crowd. It works because they know my voice so well. This didn't happen in one day. It was years of me talking to them. It's the sort of recognition we should all aspire to have with our Heavenly Father.

Regularly praying and reading the Bible daily are practical ways to learn to hear God's voice. It's learning the basic inflections and words of our God. After that, if you're not already connected to a local church, this needs to become your priority. It's a weekly space where you and others come together to hear from God and learn about his will for humanity that goes beyond individualism.

Imagine a regular Monday morning, Wednesday afternoon, or Friday night and unexpectedly hearing God say your name. This can be your reality! You stop what you're doing to discern what he is trying to tell you. In doing so, you prevent yourself from getting lost or going astray—bringing closer to God than further from him.

WHAT'RE YOU GOING TO DO ABOUT IT?

We don't only ask about what God is saying to people each Sunday. Reflection is important, but responding is equally critical. What're you going to do about what God is saying to you?

Those drifting in the church community Jude writes to might've answered the first question, but they certainly did not answer this one. There was a disconnect, a blend of intentionality and ignorance, between what they knew and what they were doing. Let's avoid making the same mistakes so we can be assured we're the group Jude is seeking to help, not rebuke. Thomas R. Schreiner comments that we:

> "Must not think the faith will be preserved simply by attacking the false teachers and revealing their errors. The readers must be attentive to their own relationship with God. They must remain in God's love by growing in their understanding of the faith, by praying fervently in the Holy Spirit, and by waiting eagerly for Jesus to return and to grant them his mercy."[13]

We're all imperfect. When a group of imperfect people gets together, they form an imperfect community. That includes the Church on this side of eternity. The foundation of our faith is that we couldn't save ourselves and needed a substantial amount of help. There's a way to respond to mistakes that better yourselves and help heal the community.

But when those mistakes become habitual, we become what Jude warns us about. We also must be aware that some people may be fraudulent. When we seek out a leader, we ought to prayerfully discern if they're in it for the right reasons. Do they point people to the lordship of Jesus or to their own authority? We can look at the fruit of someone's life, but we should also look at the fruit of our own lives.

This may require a troubling self-evaluation. Do I really submit to Jesus' authority, surrendering everything to him—or just the parts I'm okay with? Suppose we blame, instead of taking responsibility, for what we say, think, or do. In that case, we're acting like those Jude warns about. We are like spiritual imposters when we only consume instead of contributing to the church community.

This is uncomfortable. It can happen on purpose, but more often than not, it happens unintentionally. That's why Jude writes this letter. The things we say, do, and think today have eternal implications. Still, we'll find that we can be misled and misled by others.

Jude had to wonder about this after putting the final punctuation on his letter and sending it off to the original audience. What would those who receive this message do with it? Will they remember that who they are is more important than what they do because of what Jesus alone did for them? Would they step up and work toward faithfulness, generosity, justice, humility, and authenticity to combat the slow but severe deterioration of the Gospel around them? Will they reach out and help their church community?

Would they confront their reality or compromise the truth?

What will you do?

ACKNOWLEDGEMENTS

Megan. *I love you*. The journey we've been on together has been more incredible than I could have hoped for.

Mom & Dad. The values you instilled in me as a child are the values I live by today. It's impossible to imagine doing what I'm doing today without you.

Madison Church. I have the best job in the world because of you, and *Uprising* wouldn't have happened without you.

Jacob Musselman. Who knows how many hours you spent on the phone listening to me go through, in real time, all the stories I wrote about in this book. I owe you a drink.

Tyler Nylen. Thank you for inviting me into some sacred spaces that allow me to further my awareness and understanding of justice and for helping me shape *Chapters 7-8*.

Sarah Hanson. Your enthusiasm for this project was second to none. Thanks for your feedback on a few of my "bad" chapters!

Don Ruffenach, Tim Cook, Marty Mittelstadt, Josh Crain, Steven Smallwood, John Jay Wilson, Jeremy Johnson, Gayland Hendrickson, Jason Webb, Jon

Ferguson, Sam Farina, and John Davis. You all played a significant role at critical moments in my life. I'm forever grateful for your investments in me.

A special and sincere thanks to Kara Moore, Elizabeth Morrison, Trevor Stewart, Kristina Konstantinova, Rebekah Black, and the rest of the team at Equip Press for working with me to make my childhood dream of writing a book a reality.

ENDNOTES

1   Stanley, Andy. *Not In It to Win It: Why Choosing Sides Sidelines the Church*. Zondervan (2022).

2   Rowston, D.J. *The Most Neglected Book in the New Testament*. Cambridge University Press (2009).

3   Sweet, Leonard. *Red Skies: 10 Essential Conversations Exploring Our Future as The Church*. 100 Movements Publishing (2022).

4   Moo, Douglas J. *The NIV Application Commentary: 2 Peter, Jude*. Zondervan (1996).

5   Barna, *Reviving Evangelism: Current Realities That Demand a New Vision for Sharing Faith*. Barna Group (2019).

6   Witherington III, Ben. *Letters and Homilies for Jewish Christians: A Socio-Rhetorical Commentary on Hebrews, James and Jude*. InterVarsity Press (2007).

7   Mbuvi, Andrew M. *Jude & 2 Peter*. Cascade Books (2015).

8   Bauckham, Richard. *Word Biblical Commentary: Jude-2 Peter*. Zondervan (1983).

9   Perry, Jackie Hill. *Jude: Contending for The Faith in Today's Culture*. Lifeway Press (2019).

10 Wright, N.T. *The Early Christian Letters for Everyone: James, Peter, John, and Judah*. Westminster John Knox Press (2011).

11 Moo, Douglas J. *The NIV Application Commentary: 2 Peter, Jude*. Zondervan (1996).

12 Skaggs, Rebecca. *The Pentecostal Commentary on 1 Peter, 2 Peter, Jude*. T&T Clark International (2004).

13 Schreiner, Thomas R. *The New American Commentary: 1, 2 Peter, Jude*. B & H Publishing Group (2003).